This book belongs to

_____

...a woman after God's own heart.

Experiencing God's Peace

Elizabeth George

HARVEST HOUSE PUBLISHERS

EUGENE, OREGON

Cover by Dugan Design Group, Bloomington, Minnesota

Acknowledgments

How does an author ever properly and thoroughly thank a publisher for its unfailing support, unbroken encouragement, and unlimited vision? I don't know, but I do want to try. So "Thank you, dear Harvest House Publishers!" Thank you, Bob Hawkins, Jr., Carolyn McCready, LaRae Weikert, and Steve Miller. Thank you, Terry Glaspey, Barbara Sherrill, and Betty Fletcher. Thank you, Julie McKinney, Teresa Evenson, and John Constance, for getting the word out there! Thank you all for your patient assistance with my books. And now, thank you for putting wings on this Bible study series so that women can grow to know our Lord and Savior even better.

EXPERIENCING GOD'S PEACE
Copyright © 2000 Elizabeth George
Published by Harvest House Publishers
Eugene, Oregon 97402
www.harvesthousepublishers.com

ISBN 978-0-7369-0289-2

Contents

Before You Begin

1. Experiencing God's Peace 11
   —ACTS 16:6-40

2. Counting on God's Peace 18
   —PHILIPPIANS 1:1-2

3. Giving Thanks for Others 23
   —PHILIPPIANS 1:3-8

4. Praying for Others 28
   —PHILIPPIANS 1:9-11

5. Blooming Where You're Planted 33
   —PHILIPPIANS 1:12-18a

6. Living with Heaven in View 39
   —PHILIPPIANS 1:18b-26

7. Striving Together 45
   —PHILIPPIANS 1:27-30

8. Looking to the Needs of Others 51
   —PHILIPPIANS 2:1-4

9. Living Like Jesus 56
   —PHILIPPIANS 2:5-11

10. Living Like Paul 61
    —PHILIPPIANS 2:12-18

11. Living Like Timothy 66
    —PHILIPPIANS 2:19-24

12. Living Like Epaphroditus 71
    —PHILIPPIANS 2:25-30

13. Warning the Flock 77
    —PHILIPPIANS 3:1-3

14. Losing All to Gain All 83
—Philippians 3:4-7

15. Knowing God 88
—Philippians 3:8-11

16. Conquering by Continuing 92
—Philippians 3:12-14

17. Maturing in Christ 97
—Philippians 3:15-16

18. Following Those
Who Follow the Lord 102
—Philippians 3:17-21

19. Living in Unity 108
—Philippians 4:1-3

20. Overcoming Anxiety 112
—Philippians 4:4-7

21. Thinking on God's Truths 118
—Philippians 4:8-9

22. Coping with Life's Circumstances 124
—Philippians 4:10-14

23. Giving God's Way 129
—Philippians 4:15-19

24. Beginnings and Endings 134
—Philippians 4:20-23

25. Looking Back...and Moving Forward 139
—Philippians Review

How to Study the Bible 143

Leading a Bible Study Discussion Group 148

Notes 155

Bibliography 157

Foreword

For some time I have been looking for Bible studies that I could use each day that would increase my knowledge of God's Word. In my search, I found myself struggling between two extremes: Bible studies that required little time but also had little substance, or studies that were in-depth and demanded more time than I could give. I discovered that I wasn't alone—there were many other women like me who were busy yet desired to spend quality time studying God's Word.

That's why I became excited when Elizabeth George shared her desire to create a series of women's Bible studies that offered in-depth lessons that could be completed in just 15-20 minutes per day. When she completed the first study—on Philippians—I was eager to try it out. I had already studied Philippians many times, but this was the first time I had come to understand exactly how the whole book fit together and how it can truly be lived out in my life. Each lesson was simple but insightful—and was written especially to apply to me as a woman!

In the Woman After God's Own Heart Bible study series, Elizabeth takes you step by step through the Scriptures, sharing wisdom she has gleaned from more than 20 years as a women's Bible teacher. The lessons are rich and meaningful because they're rooted in God's Word and have been lived out in Elizabeth's life. Her thoughtful and personable guidance make you feel as though you are studying right alongside her—as if she is personally mentoring you in the greatest aspiration you could ever pursue: to become a woman after God's own heart.

If you're looking for Bible studies that can help you grow stronger in your knowledge of God's Word even in the most demanding of schedules, I know you'll find this series to be a welcome companion in your daily walk with God.

—LaRae Weikert
Vice President, Editorial
Harvest House Publishers

Before You Begin

In my book *A Woman After God's Own Heart,* I describe such a woman as one who ensures that God is first in her heart and the Ultimate Priority of her life. Then I share that one crucial way this desire can become reality is by nurturing a heart that abides in God's Word. To do so means that you and I must develop a root system anchored deep in God's Word.

Before you launch into this Bible study, take a moment to think about these aspects of a root system produced by the regular, faithful study of God's Word:

- *Roots are unseen*—You'll want to set aside time in solitude— "underground" if you will—to immerse yourself in God's Word and grow in Him.

- *Roots are for taking in*—Alone and with your Bible in hand, you'll want to take in and feed upon the truths of the Word of God and ensure your spiritual growth.

- *Roots are for storage*—As you form the habit of looking into God's Word, you'll find a vast, deep reservoir of divine hope and strength forming for the rough times.

- *Roots are for support*—Do you want to stand strong in the Lord? To stand firm against the pressures of life? The routine care of your roots through exposure to God's Word will cultivate you into a remarkable woman of endurance.[1]

I'm glad you've chosen this study out of my A Woman After God's Own Heart Bible Study Series. My prayer for you is that the truths you find in God's Word through this study will further transform your life into the image of His dear Son and empower you to be the woman you seek to be: a woman after God's own heart.

In His love,

Elizabeth George

esson 1

Experiencing God's Peace

Acts 16:6-40

eace. There are many means by which we try to bring about the peace our souls so long for! We purchase tranquil paintings meant to evoke a sense of peace. We buy music that can help us to relax. In home gardens, shopping malls, and parks we build waterfalls, pools, ponds, and fountains to summon up feelings of peace. We also equate early morning and evening with peace and quiet. And we're told that sitting in the sun releases vitamin D into our systems, helping us to relax!

But our wonderful God has provided real peace for us as His dear children—and this includes you! What a splendid thought to know that, even though Jesus stated, "In the world you will have tribulation" (John 16:33), you have the provision of God's perfect peace in every circumstance through all of life.

As we think about experiencing God's peace, it's appropriate for us to turn to the tiny New Testament book of Philippians, which talks about peace. The apostle Paul wrote this small epistle to his beloved friends in Philippi. Let's begin by seeing how the church at Philippi came to be.

Out of God's Word...

1. Quickly read Acts 16:6-40. Here, we meet Paul on his second missionary journey. What do you learn about how his steps were ordered as he attempted to preach the gospel (verses 6-7)?

   The holy spirit was prompting Paul not to teach the gospel.

   How was he led to the city of Philippi?

   Paul had a vision.

2. Beginning at verse 13, note these details about a significant meeting:
   Who was present? *women*

   When and where was it held? *the Sabboth at the riverbank*
   And what was the purpose of the meeting?
   Prayer

3. Describe the character and events surrounding Lydia, a significant woman (verses 14-15).
   She opened her heart to the Lord and she was babtized with her family.

4. Now describe the events surrounding Paul's encounter with a female fortune teller (verses 16-18).
   She was demon possed slave girl. Paul command the demon to come out of her in the name of Jesus Christ and it instantly left her

Give a brief account of what happened to Paul and his friend Silas afterward (verses 19-24). *They were severely beaten and thrown into prison for teaching the gospel.*

How did they handle their painful and difficult circumstances (verse 25)? *They prayed and sang hymns to God.*

5. Note the actions of the Philippian jailer:
   His charge (verse 23)? *He was ordered to make sure they didn't escape.*

   His response to his charge (verse 24)? *He put them in the dungeon and clamped their feet.*

   His response to the earthquake (verse 27)? *He thought the prisoners had escaped so he was about to kill himself.*

   His response to Paul's cry (verses 28-30)? *He asked what he needed to do to be saved.*

   His response to the gospel (verses 31-34)? *He had them to his household & fed them, he & his house were baptized.*

6. Finally, note where the new church at Philippi probably met (verse 40). *At Lydia's house*

...*and into your heart*

Dear one, these few scriptures from God's Holy Word give us much to reflect upon! For instance,

- Think about how you normally respond when your plans and dreams are thwarted. How does Paul's refusal to give up his efforts to preach the gospel point you to better ways of responding to life's denials?

- And how does the fact of God's intervention and leading in the life of Paul change your view of the things that "happen" to you along life's way?

*C*ommenting on what happened to Paul and Silas, pastor and teacher G. Campbell Morgan writes that they "were guided by hindrance.... The lesson we are to learn is that of the importance of obedience to the guidance of the Spirit when we cannot understand the reason, and indeed when it seems to us that the way marked out is preventing us from fulfilling the highest things of our most sacred calling. The experience is not rare. Over and over again in the path of true service we are brought to just such places. A great opportunity is open right before us, and we are not permitted to avail ourselves of it. Or we are in the midst of work which is full of real success, and we are called to abandon it. We should never hesitate. This wonderful page of apostolic history teaches us that God's outlook is greater and grander than our own. We may always leave the issue to Him, and presently we shall learn how wise His way, how strong His will."[2]

- Looking next to Lydia, what impresses you the most about her? What actions can you take today to follow in her steps?

> $\mathcal{H}$ear the words of another regarding our friend Lydia: "Lydia's response to the gospel was personal, profound, and practical. She opened her own life to Jesus. She then led her entire household in committing themselves to Christ in baptism. Then she insisted on having the missionaries make her house their base of operation...
>
> "To the extent that Lydia understood God, she obeyed. She displayed a willing heart. When God showed her more, she immediately responded. Does your plan and schedule for today reflect your desire to respond to God wherever you may be?"[3]
>
> *—365 Life Lessons from Bible People*

- Think a moment about the Philippian jailer. What were the evidences that his faith was genuine?

Take to heart these facts about the Philippian jailer...and make each one your own:

First, he was afraid he would lose his life!

Then, he was afraid he would lose his soul!

Finally, he was blessed all around:

> His life was spared.
>
> His soul was secured.
>
> His family was saved.
>
> His compassion was stirred.

Heart Response

As I step back and try to take in the whole of Acts 16 and all that Paul and Silas endured in the process of starting up the Philippian church, I can't help but liken it to childbirth. Just as bringing a dear, sweet baby into this world calls for tremendous responsibility and commitment on the part of the mother, giving birth to the church at Philippi required much from Paul and Silas. Just as there is great pleasure mixed with pain in childbirth, Paul and Silas experienced joy and sorrow.

See if you can, for a moment, put yourself into their shoes. Paul and Silas encountered some wonderful people—like Lydia and the band of ladies who worshiped by the river. But then, too, there were the not-so-nice people like the demon-possessed woman and the town folk who mistreated

Paul and Silas. There was also the jailer, who initially seemed to fall into the not-so-nice category, but in the end believed, along with his entire family, and was used by God to bless Paul and Silas with physical care.

Yes, these servants of God went through many difficulties and much pain and discomfort along their path toward God's will. Yet, in the end, the precious Philippian church was born. I hope you'll remember this comparison to physical childbirth whenever you, too, dear one, encounter pain and face perplexing obstacles and closed doors along *your* path.

I find it amazing that never once in this saga of suffering do we see Paul and Silas stopping, quitting, having a fit, exploding, emoting, complaining, sinking into depression, ranting, raving, or resigning from the Christian race and their mission. No, they were persistent and consistent. Regardless of their predicament, they appear to have learned to be content in all their circumstances (Philippians 4:11-13). They looked to the Savior for His strength and went on, pressed on, and kept on seeking the will of the Lord. They served Him wholeheartedly (no matter what the cost!), enduring affliction, and trusting the Lord and His purposes.

As Paul wrote elsewhere, "Therefore, my beloved brethren, be steadfast, immovable, always abounding in the work of the Lord, knowing that your labor is not in vain in the Lord" (1 Corinthians 15:58). May we look to the Lord, look to His faithful servants Paul and Silas, and keep on keeping on! I pray we learn these lessons well, for then we will experience the peace we long for—God's peace, and His manifold blessings!

esson 2

Counting on God's Peace

*H*ave you ever been separated from someone you dearly love and long to communicate with? That's the situation Paul was in when it came to his beloved friends at Philippi. That's why he took pen in hand and wrote the epistle of Philippians. I'm sure you've written many letters for the same reason, but there was one highly unusual fact about Paul's letter—it was written while he was imprisoned under house arrest in Rome (Acts 28:30)! In fact, he was awaiting Caesar's verdict, which could mean execution—making his little letter all the more urgent!

What was it Paul wanted to say to the Philippians? Well, he most definitely wanted to *express his love to them*. He also wanted to *thank them*. You see, this church body had sent Paul money (Philippians 4:15), and they had also sent him

Epaphroditus, a member from their own congregation, to help him (2:25). Paul also wanted to *comfort the church* at Philippi. They were greatly worried about his imprisonment and possible execution; and they were deeply concerned about their friend Epaphroditus, who had been deathly ill (2:27). Paul also wanted to *warn and correct them* about a few things. And so Paul begins:

Philippians 1:1-2

¹ Paul and Timothy, servants of Jesus Christ, to all the saints in Christ Jesus who are in Philippi, with the bishops and deacons:

² Grace to you and peace from God our Father and the Lord Jesus Christ.

Out of God's Word...

1. First note how Paul and Timothy describe themselves (verse 1).

   Servants of Jesus Christ

   To what three groups of people in the Philippian church is their letter addressed (verse 1)? *all the saints in Jesus Chris, bishops & deacons*

2. Next, list the two spiritual blessings that come to all believers in Christ (verse 2).

   Grace and peace

3. In a word or two, how would you describe the general tone of Paul's letter to this point?

...and into your heart

- Don't you find it amazing that a great leader like the apostle Paul and his right-hand man, Timothy, chose to evaluate and describe themselves as "servants" of Jesus Christ? The Greek word Paul used for "servant" was doulos, which refers to a slave who had no will, no rights, and no possessions of his or her own. Instead, he was the possession of another...forever! A slave's role in life was singular: To obey his or her master's will quickly, quietly, and without question.

  What is your evaluation of yourself? For instance, if you were asked to introduce yourself to others, how would you choose to describe yourself? Or, put another way, what is the most important aspect of your life? Jot down your answers in a sentence or two.

  Do your answers reveal the need for changes in attitude so that you, too, may proclaim along with Paul and Timothy, "I am a servant, a slave, a handmaiden, a doulos of Jesus Christ"? Note at least one change you will make.

- Moving from slaves to saints, consider that a saint is someone who has been set apart by the Lord to glorify Him. A saint is a holy one, meaning set apart and consecrated unto the service of God.

  In your own words, write a sentence about what it means to be holy and set apart unto God—Like Paul and Timothy.

  Again, are there changes you can make? Note at least one here.

• Think again about the twin resources of God's grace and God's peace, which Paul says are ours as God's women.

God's grace—God's grace is His unmerited favor poured out upon those who have trusted in Jesus Christ. But did you know that the whole sustaining power of God is packaged within His grace and favor? God's grace means God's force and His power. It's God's marvelous grace that enables us to go from strength to strength (Psalm 84:7) through all the trials of life. And, just as God is all that you need, so God's grace is also all that you need it to be. It is truly sufficient (see 2 Corinthians 12:9).

God's peace—As one of God's children, you, my friend, can enjoy a childlike confidence and trust and hope in the Lord. Truly you have peace with God, the peace of God, and the God of peace (see Philippians 4:7,9)—all you need for total well-being!

What does God's Word say about how you can experience God's grace and God's peace? Or, share one of your favorite scriptures about peace.

First: Identify your most pressing trial or difficulty for this day.

Second: Purpose to tap into these two supernatural resources—God's power and God's peace. They are all yours if you belong to the family of God through Jesus Christ, and they are readily available. Be specific about how and when you'll look to the Lord for these means.

Heart Response

My heart is soaring! Why? Because in just 37 words Paul's pen touches (perhaps pierces...?) the heart of every woman after God's own heart! The tri-fold challenge of truly being a *servant*, a *saint*, and the possessor of His *supernatural resources* of grace and peace is so consuming that I'm glad we only attempted to grasp these two brief verses here at the beginning of our walk toward experiencing God's peace. I know that I truly want to be a servant of the Lord Most High, one who has no other master (and no other life!) but Him, one who is completely "sold out." And I also yearn to be set apart. Holiness is something I think long and hard about and pray fervently for. I believe this calling from God to a sold-out and set-apart lifestyle should cause you and me, as God's women, to search and "examine ourselves" (2 Corinthians 13:5). We must look to the Holy Spirit (Galatians 5:16) and the Word of God to discover what is unholy and unpleasing to our Master. And most certainly we ought to remember (even more often) to look to the Lord and count upon His grace and power in every situation. It's there, dear friend! It's given. It's provided. And it brings with it the peace we so long for. I'm glad we stopped briefly in these first two verses to look at such life-changing truths!

Lesson 3

Giving Thanks for Others

Philippians 1:3-8

Imagine sitting in chains...alone...apart from those you know...away from those you love...and awaiting a verdict that will determine whether you live or die. These lonely and potentially fear-provoking conditions describe Paul's situation as we look at today's lesson. And yet Paul realized complete peace as he turned his thoughts and soul and prayers heavenward, and thought of others instead of himself.

This same remarkable peace can be yours, too, as you go through any difficulty. Many women sit alone—some for days, some for nights, and some for days and nights on end. Many of us are forced to spend large amounts of time apart and away from friends and loved ones. And countless others sit awaiting verdicts (from cancer tests, from lawyers, from

spouses, from employers) that will point their life in new and oftentimes uncertain directions.

Aren't you glad that God's Word shows us—in the grievous circumstances of the apostle Paul's life—a marvelous way to experience God's perfect peace even in the midst of our problems? Take note of the three perspectives that brought great joy and peace of mind to Paul. And remember...they will do the same for you!

Philippians 1:3-8

3 I thank my God upon every remembrance of you,

4 always in every prayer of mine making request for you all with joy,

5 for your fellowship in the gospel from the first day until now,

6 being confident of this very thing, that He who has begun a good work in you will complete it until the day of Jesus Christ;

7 just as it is right for me to think this of you all, because I have you in my heart, inasmuch as both in my chains and in the defense and confirmation of the gospel, you all are partakers with me of grace.

8 For God is my witness, how greatly I long for you all with the affection of Jesus Christ.

Out of God's Word...

1. What does Paul do when he remembers the Philippian believers (verse 3)?

How does he pray for these people who are so far away (verses 4-6)?

Verse 4—With

Verse 5—For

Verse 6—With

2. What do you learn about the character of God in verse 6?

3. How would you describe Paul's feelings toward his fellow believers (verses 7-8)?

...and into your heart

As I mentioned earlier, three wonderful perspectives helped provide Paul with peace of mind.

- *A Positive Attitude:*
  How do you normally think of others? Are you positive? Petty? Picky? Gracious? Jot down the traits that generally describe your thoughts.

Now, do you need to make a conscious effort to nurture a more positive attitude toward others? Scan through Philippians 1:3-8 again and quickly note a few practices or perspectives from Paul's heart that will help you.

- *A Promise to Claim*
  Write out verse 6 here:

In a word or two, what effect did this promise have on Paul in his situation?

And how did this promise affect the thoughts Paul had about the people he was writing to—people who were so far away, people he might never see again?

Do you know a precious Christian who is far away from you, either physically or emotionally or spiritually? How can the promise from verse 6 give you peace of mind?

- *A Passionate Heart*
  What does verse 8 reveal about Paul's heart toward those he knew, and how can you cultivate such a heart?

Heart Response

Oh, that we would learn Paul's formula for peace, and learn it well! In his awful circumstances he could experience the peace of God as he concerned himself with others. You see, he had *a positive attitude, a promise from God* to claim, and *a passionate heart*.

And Paul did another thing: He looked to God, our wonderful God who is the author and perfecter and finisher of all He begins, our omniscient God who sees the end product as perfect and complete! God saw the people in Paul's life as they *would* be, and Paul sought to do the same. We, too, can rest in the same fact—that God sees those in our lives (ourselves included!) as they (and we) *will* be!

So, beloved, to experience the power of peace in every situation, begin with thanksgiving. Did you know that the giving of thanks is willful? It's a decision on our part. And giving thanks is also commanded by God. His Word tells us to give thanks *always* and for *all* things, in *everything* and *evermore* (see Ephesians 5:20; 1 Thessalonians 5:16,18). And the decision to do just that—to give thanks, no matter what (or in what situation)—has a powerful effect on our attitude...and our peace.

"The peace of God, which surpasses all understanding" (Philippians 4:7) is indeed available to you and me. Why not give thanks for this fact?

Lesson 4

Praying for Others

Philippians 1:9-11

Every Christian woman prays for those whom she loves and cares about. Yet it's easy to fall into a pattern of praying for the *temporal* things in the lives of those we cherish. It doesn't take much thought to ask God to bless others financially or to resolve their health concerns. Almost without effort we can find ourselves praying in a routine sort of way for our children's friends or for fellow believers looking for a place to live, selecting a college, or seeking a job. Then there are the habitual prayers for the little daily things in life—for parking places, for bargains, for our children to nap well, for safety for one more day.

But God's faithful servant Paul shows us a more significant way to pray for those we know and love. As you ponder Philippians 1:9-11 and the content of Paul's prayer for his beloved Philippian friends, remember the situation in his own life at the time. Paul is a prisoner awaiting his sentence. However, rather than brood over his personal problems, Paul experiences God's peace as he thinks about others. That brings us to the content of his prayers on behalf of those in Philippi. It's hardly what we would call a "baby prayer," a prayer for health, wealth, and happiness. No, Paul prays an "adult prayer" for his beloved friends—the prayer of a man who knows what truly matters in a life and a soul.

Read…and relish…and remember this exceptional prayer for the things of true substance for those Paul loved. Listen as he lifts their lives before God Almighty.

Philippians 1:9-11

⁹ And this I pray, that your love may abound still more and more in knowledge and all discernment,

¹⁰ that you may approve the things that are excellent, that you may be sincere and without offense till the day of Christ,

¹¹ being filled with the fruits of righteousness which are by Jesus Christ, to the glory and praise of God.

Out of God's Word…

1. What is Paul's first request on behalf of the Philippians (verse 9)?

   And what two qualities does he desire for them in this area (verse 9)?

2. In what two ways will the approval of things that are excellent affect us here and now (verse 10)?

3. State the source of the fruits of righteousness (verse 11).

Note also the end result of these fruits (verse 11).

4. Fill in these blanks: Paul prays...

THAT the Philippians' _____ would _____
with more _____ and_____
SO THAT they would approve things _____
SO THAT they would be _____ and _____
SO THAT they would bring _____ and_____
to God.

5. In just a few words, what is the content of Paul's prayer for his friends?

...*and into your heart*

Paul's words not only apply to our prayers for others, but also to the prayers we say for ourselves.

- *Regarding others*—Based on Paul's prayer for the Philippians, what adjustments can you make in the content of your prayers on behalf of those you know and love?

- *Regarding yourself*—What aspect of Paul's prayer for excellence in spiritual things could you concentrate on for greater growth in your own life as a Christian?

- *Regarding others and yourself*—Don't forget to pray for knowledge and discernment! Love is not merely emotion. What will *you* do to grow in knowledge and discernment?

- *Regarding prayer*—It's worthy to consider the nature and content of our prayers for others and for ourselves. But, if you and I are not women of prayer, the lofty substance of Paul's prayer here in Philippians 1:9-11 will never be uttered on behalf of the lives of God's people. Please take to heart this thought about the importance of prayer compared to the many other "things" we tend to do with our time.

*I*f we are willing to spend hours on end to learn to play the piano, operate a computer, or fly an airplane, it is sheer nonsense for us to imagine that we can learn the high art of getting guidance through communion with the Lord without being willing to set aside time for it. It is no accident that the Bible speaks of prayer as a form of *waiting* on God.[4]

—**Paul Rees**

When will you pray, dear one? Note a time here...and then *pray!*

Heart Response

And this I pray, dear friend and sister in Christ, for you and me:

I pray that we would learn the discipline of lifting our thoughts and our prayers, our aims and our lives, heaven-ward, upward, far above and beyond that which is routine and mundane.

I pray that we would grow to become women of prayer—with regular, daily, unhurried, secret lingerings in prayer.

I pray that others might be encouraged by knowing that we pray for them, and by knowing *what* we pray for them.

I pray that we would pray as Paul prayed, using these three sweet-but-packed verses as our guide to praying for others.

I pray that our lives would bring great glory and praise to our Lord Jesus Christ and God, our Father; that our lives would be filled with the fruits of righteousness, fruit—abundant fruit spilling forth to bless others and to reflect well upon our Savior.

I pray that we will remember the thoughts and truths of Paul's prayer.

Amen.

Blooming Where You're Planted

Philippians 1:12-18a

*M*ost people, when they think of their lifetime goals, envision a future filled with security, ease, longevity, and wealth—the good life. This worldly good life, however, was not the case for God's bond-servant Paul. In Lesson 6 we'll see Paul declare, "For to me, to live is Christ" (Philippians 1:21). For Paul there was no other option but to spend his life in full-out sacrificial service.

But for now, for today, let's look at one of Paul's secrets to peace. Let's see exactly how he enjoyed an abundance of God's peace, even in the midst of what looked like a tragedy. As you read through this precious passage of Scripture, note the many ways Paul "bloomed where he was planted"— even when he was "planted" in prison!

33

Philippians 1:12-18a

¹² But I want you to know, brethren, that the things which happened to me have actually turned out for the furtherance of the gospel,

¹³ so that it has become evident to the whole palace guard, and to all the rest, that my chains are in Christ;

¹⁴ and most of the brethren in the Lord, having become confident by my chains, are much more bold to speak the word without fear.

¹⁵ Some indeed preach Christ even from envy and strife, and some also from good will:

¹⁶ The former preach Christ from selfish ambition, not sincerely, supposing to add affliction to my chains;

¹⁷ but the latter out of love, knowing that I am appointed for the defense of the gospel.

¹⁸ What then? Only that in every way, whether in pretense or in truth, Christ is preached; and in this I rejoice....

Out of God's Word...

1. Perhaps imagining that his friends might have heard he was suffering as a prisoner in bonds, Paul turns from greetings (verses 1-11) to a "mission update." What is the first thing he wants the readers of his "newsletter," the epistle of Philippians, to know about his imprisonment (verse 12)?

What is Paul's personal condition (verse 13)?

Who is his audience (verse 13)?

2. Continuing to let his friends know what is going on in his life, Paul describes the two groups who are preaching the gospel of Christ during Paul's absence due to imprisonment. Scan verses 15-17 again and, in a few words, describe the groups and their differing approaches to sharing the gospel.

Paul's friends:

Paul's enemies:

3. Even though these two groups differed in their motives and means of sharing the good news of Jesus Christ, what was the singular outcome (verse 18)?

And what was Paul's attitude about this outcome (verse 18)?

...and into your heart

- Paul's outlook on his situation, despite his bonds and imprisonment and removal from public ministry, was overwhelmingly positive. His final statement about his divinely appointed circumstances and God's use of them was, "In this I rejoice" (verse 18). Here are some of the "good" outcomes from Paul's "bad" situation:

—Paul enjoyed a powerful personal witness to the elite Roman guard (verse 13). He was always chained to a member of the Praetorian Guard, the Imperial Guard of Rome. Every six hours his guard changed. That's 365 days a year, for two years. At four guards a day, Paul had 2,920 opportunities to share one-on-one about Jesus! Perhaps some of these soldiers who were sent throughout the Roman Empire spread the message of Jesus Christ they had heard from the lips of the prisoner Paul. What a ministry!—one Paul would not have had were he not under their guard.

—Paul the prisoner suddenly found time to write this marvelous and uplifting epistle that blessed the Philippian church and extends the blessing of encouragement to us today. The four sparkling chapters of this little book have brought joy, faith, hope, love, and peace to Christians for almost 2,000 years!

—Because Paul preached the gospel in his bonds (verse 13), others were inspired to join him in proclamation. His bonds also gave him access to the flower of the Roman army, but his absence created a need (and an opportunity!) for others to step in and fill the vacuum.

—Regardless of how or why the gospel was preached or who preached it, in every way, Christ was preached (verse 18).

—Even as a prisoner, Paul experienced God's peace and joy (verse 18).

• And now for you and your life, my friend. To whom or to what are you "chained"? Or, put another way, what are your divinely appointed circumstances? For instance, are you a wife, a mother, a single, a widow, a homemaker, an employee? Jot a quick answer here.

• Paul has often been referred to as "the optimistic prisoner." In his evaluation, the things that happened to him actually turned out for good (verse 12). What lesson about suffering and difficulty can you draw from Paul's attitude?

Also name one constructive or positive thing you can do today in your situation.

Heart Response

Well, dear one, where does today find you? How I would love to know your answers to the questions above!

But I want to leave you with yet a few more words—powerful words—from the pen of Paul. He wrote these uplifting lines in Romans 8:28-29: "And we know that all things work together for good to those who love God, to those who are the called according to His purpose. For whom He foreknew, He also predestined to be conformed to the image of His Son...."

Beloved, our knowing God and trusting in His promise to work all things together for good makes us women of hope. Our God is in control of *all* things—even those things that appear to be negative—and He will work all things for our good and for His purposes. And, as another has noted:

> *M*any a great Christian was molded in character in the crucible of suffering, matured in loneliness, and prepared for greater usefulness in God's hands than if untouched by the storms of life.[5]
>
> —John F. Walvoord

When we choose to bloom where our all-wise God plants us, we, too, will one day be able to declare with Paul, "But I want you to know, brethren, that the things which happened to me have actually turned out for the furtherance of the gospel.... I want you to know that God has worked all things together for His good purposes!"

Living with Heaven in View

Philippians 1:18b-26

*H*ave you visited a bookstore lately? If so, I'm sure you've seen the sections crammed with best-selling self-help and "how-to" books—all with step-by-step directions for achieving just about anything you can think of.

But do you see many books titled *How to Die,* or *Your Guide to Dying?* I doubt it. I know I haven't. It's not a popular (or comfortable!) subject. Desperate for an answer, a small child wrote, "Dear God, What is it like when you die? Nobody will tell me. I just want to know. I don't want to do it!" Adults are not so brave to ask. No, we'd rather search for the how-to's of living the good life!

But, my sister in Christ, God's suffering servant Paul gives us *both* answers. In these eight-plus verses, Paul shows us not only how to live, but also how to die. In both life...and death...Paul is a "saint," one dedicated to the service of the Lord—to Him and to His people. It's very likely that Paul thought about death each and every day as he waited for a verdict that could mean life or death. In these verses we hear Paul's musings and prayers reflecting his outlook on both life *and* death. Let's see what conclusions he came to.

Philippians 1:18b-26

18 ...yes, and will rejoice.

19 For I know that this will turn out for my salvation through your prayer and the supply of the Spirit of Jesus Christ,

20 according to my earnest expectation and hope that in nothing I shall be ashamed, but that with all boldness, as always, so now also Christ will be magnified in my body, whether by life or by death.

21 For to me, to live is Christ, and to die is gain.

22 But if I live on in the flesh, this will mean fruit from my labor; yet what I shall choose I cannot tell.

23 For I am hard pressed between the two, having a desire to depart and be with Christ, which is far better.

24 Nevertheless to remain in the flesh is more needful for you.

25 And being confident of this, I know that I shall remain and continue with you all for your progress and joy of faith,

26 that your rejoicing for me may be more abundant in Jesus Christ by my coming to you again.

Out of God's Word...

1. What is Paul's concern in either life or death (verse 20)?

2. Looking at verse 21, how does Paul, the "sold-out" apostle, view life?

   And death?

3. If he lives, what will that mean for Paul and the Philippians according to

   verse 22?

   verse 24?

   verse 25?

   verse 26?

4. With what does Paul equate death in verse 23?

How does death compare with life (verse 23)?

One Bible teacher gives us this visual aid for contrasting life and death:[6]

Remaining here	*Departing to be with Christ*
A temporary residence, a mere tent dwelling	A permanent abode
Suffering mixed with joy	Joy unmixed with suffering
Suffering for a little while	Joy forever
Being absent from the Lord	Being at home with the Lord
The fight	The feast
The realm of sin	The realm of complete deliverance from sin

...*and into your heart*

- Regarding death:
  How do you think most people view death?

What new truths have you learned from this passage?

When English Puritan Richard Baxter lay dying at age 76, racked with pain and disease, a friend asked him, "Dear Mr. Baxter, how are you?" His reply? "Almost well!" What a perspective! Mr. Baxter knew—and believed—that death meant simply to depart and be with Jesus, which is far better. Or, as another has said of death and dying, "God is stripping me of everything to give me everything." No, death is not the end, not the unknown, not the worst thing that can happen to us. As a line of poetry reads, "Better, far better with Christ to be, living and loved through eternity."

Oh, how Paul loved the Lord! And, oh, how Paul yearned to be with the Lord he loved! Yet he subordinated his personal desire to his pastoral responsibility. He chose to use his days on earth so others might know Christ.

• Regarding life:
How do you think most people view life?

What new truths have you learned from this passage?

The Bible tells us that Christ is exalted in our body as long as we live (verse 20). It also tells us "for if we live, we live to the Lord" (Romans 14:8). Life for Paul, above all, meant more ministry, more time to teach and serve others, more time for fruitful labor. May that be so for us! Richard Baxter, whom we just observed facing death at age 76, suffered ill health for 56 years prior to his passing and was once imprisoned for 18 months. And yet, like Paul, he viewed every day of life as an opportunity to minister. Like Paul, he preached every day as a dying man to dying men, never sure if he would preach again And, like Paul, he wrote, becoming one of the most voluminous of English authors, penning more than 100 works.

Heart Response

Won't you join with countless others and make this key verse to Philippians, verse 21, your creed...for life and death? Won't you join with fellow believers—like writers and missionaries Elisabeth Elliot, Carol Talbot, and Corrie ten Boom—who live and lived by these inspired words of Paul: "For to me, to live is Christ, and to die is gain"? These ladies, dear friend, are part of the great cloud of witnesses who show us how to live and how to die. Each gives and gave selflessly from her waning strength, some even tottering while teaching, but nevertheless, teaching, that they might bear more fruit in ministry and that others—like you and me—might progress and taste greater joy of faith.

Life is more than planning for retirement, saving money, purchasing a recreational vehicle, traveling, sliding for home, and living it up. Hear the prayer of Jim Elliot, the martyred first husband of Elisabeth Elliot:

> *G*od makes His ministers a flame of fire. Am I ignitable? God, deliver me from the dread asbestos of "other things." Saturate me with the oil of Thy Spirit that I may be a flame. Make me Thy fuel, Flame of God.[7]
>
> —Jim Elliot

Striving Together

Philippians 1:27-30

*W*ebster's dictionary defines a mentor as "a wise and faithful counselor." We have all faced situations and decisions that call for the advice and admonition of a wise and faithful counselor, but finding such a mentor is not an easy task. Where can we turn?

In Paul we find such a mentor, one who is faithful to point us to the conduct of a "worthy walk." He tells it to us like it is. For instance, just think about what we learned from Paul in our last lesson. Who else has ever talked about these vital real life issues of life and death in a way that makes so much sense, brings such joy, and motivates such useful productivity?

I know the book of Philippians is usually thought of as a book of joy and peace (and that's true!), but Paul also has a hard lesson in "real life" to teach the Philippians and us. It's straightforward and to the point—and it has to do with suffering, another unpopular topic! Yet Paul, the prisoner of the Lord and a role model in suffering, who was in bonds at the time he wrote these words, speaks straight to the issue. It's as if he's saying, "Let me tell you how to suffer, how to endure, what to think while you're going through it, and how to make it through triumphantly...and experience God's peace in the process!"

Wouldn't you like to have a mentor like Paul? Well, you can. Pay close attention to his wise and faithful counsel:

Philippians 1:27-30

27 Only let your conduct be worthy of the gospel of Christ, so that whether I come and see you or am absent, I may hear of your affairs, that you stand fast in one spirit, with one mind striving together for the faith of the gospel,

28 and not in any way terrified by your adversaries, which is to them a proof of perdition, but to you of salvation, and that from God.

29 For to you it has been granted on behalf of Christ, not only to believe in Him, but also to suffer for His sake,

30 having the same conflict which you saw in me and now hear is in me.

Out of God's Word...

1. So far this has been a positive letter, hasn't it? But finally, 27 verses into his thoughts, Paul gives his first word of admonition (verse 27).

What is it?

Why does he give this instruction?

2. What attitude did Paul urge the Philippians to have toward one another (verse 27)?

And toward their opponents (verse 28)?

3. What two "privileges" does Paul guarantee to believers in Jesus Christ (verse 29)?

4. Who is suffering in verse 29?

And in verse 30?

...*and into your heart*

Have you ever heard about the process that makes Dresden china so exquisite and so desirable? Well, it's the fire. This magnificent porcelain, the world's finest, is fired three times—in a process that brings out the gold and the crimson more beautifully and permanently fuses them to the china.

In a similar way the Christian is refined by fire, dear friend. There are some "privileges" that come to Christians who faithfully follow Jesus. One, Paul says, is *belief.* And the other is *suffering.* This reality could also be stated in this way: "To believe *is* to suffer!" It's sort of a "double blessing," if you will. Paul tells us elsewhere that "all who desire to live godly in Christ Jesus *will* suffer persecution" (2 Timothy 3:12, emphasis added).

So then, how are we to suffer? What does our mentor Paul have to say on this experience he was so familiar with?

- *Stand firm,* or stand fast (verse 27). This is the correct posture for suffering. We are not to be sitting, slouching, leaning, or lying down. Oh no! We are to stand firm. No backing down, and no wavering allowed!

  How's your posture when it comes to suffering? And how does verse 27 encourage you? Instruct you?

- *Strive together* (verse 27). Pain and suffering and persecution *should* come from outside the body of Christ— not from the inside. Our quarrels should not be among ourselves. Instead, Christians are to strive together, fighting side-by-side, taking a bold stand against the enemies of the cross of Christ (3:18).

  Do you know where to draw the battle lines in your relationships? Are you bogged down in doing battle with other believers? As a member of Christ's church, are you willing to change any wrong attitude that is keeping you from unity with other believers?

- *Shun fear* (verse 28). Paul says we are not to be afraid when we suffer persecution and mistreatment. Commenting on verse 28, Matthew Henry echoes Paul's advice with these words: "We need not look upon those enemies with fear whom God looks upon with contempt."[8] As you look to the Lord in your suffering and remain strong in Him, standing firm, striving together, and shunning fear, your salvation and your enemies' lack of salvation will become obvious to all.

You can take courage from this real-life story of how a strong faith in the face of suffering lived out Paul's words in verse 28:

*M*issionaries Reverend and Mrs. R.W. Porteous were taken prisoners in the spring of 1931 by communist bandits in China. After leading the pair to a lonely spot on top of a hill, the commanding officer said, "This is the place." The executioner took a knife from its holder, and raised it above the necks of the courageous couple. Certain death seemed imminent.

However, instead of cringing and begging for mercy, the husband and wife began to sing:

> Face to face with Christ, my Savior,
> Face to face—what will it be?
> When with rapture I behold Him,
> Jesus Christ who died for me.

No order was given for their death. Instead, the executioner returned the sword to its sheath, and the Porteouses were released.[9]

Heart Response

As I said earlier, it's sobering *and* inspiring when we see Christians face suffering with the proper conduct—standing firm, striving together, and shunning fear. How do they remain steadfast in their conduct? I believe one key to their exemplary behavior is faith. A strong faith stands us well in persecution, too. Just as an athlete strengthens his muscles through the discipline of a regular regimem, so you and I can nurture a stronger faith that will enable us to exhibit the conduct that is worthy of Christ. How?

1. Read God's Word regularly. It heralds the faith of those who have gone before us.

2. Pray for greater faith. The disciples boldly asked Jesus to increase their faith (Luke 17:5).

3. Read the biographies of those who have gone before us in church history. Dr. Louis Talbot, founder of Biola University and Talbot Theological Seminary, kept a copy of *Foxes' Book of Martyrs* on his bedstand and read about one martyr's death each night.

4. Ask God for "more fire." In the year 1555, two Protestant bishops were martyred for Christ at Oxford University. As Bishop Nicholas Ridley burned at the stake, he was heard calling out through the flames, "for Christ's sake, more fire!"[10]

We all need to ask God for more fire, don't we? Through the refining fire, our commitment to Christ will be deepened, our faith will be strengthened, our passion to live for Him will be ignited, and our conduct will be worthy. Seek it today...and everyday, and let's strive together until we see Him face to face!

Looking to the Needs
of Others

Philippians 2:1-4

For several years my husband's office door at The Master's Seminary displayed a cartoon that depicts the expectations of many who attend church. As the preacher in the picture mounted the platform and prepared to preach, he faced his congregation. Those sitting in front of him wore expectant expressions, and their thoughts were verbalized in the familiar bubble format above each head. One by one their thoughts went like this: "Feed me!" "Encourage me!" "Teach me!" "Love me!" "Lead me!" "Comfort me!" "Disciple me!" "Sympathize with me!" "Support me!" "Understand me!" "Pamper me!" "Stroke me!" Each and every person present had "needs," and each and every person present expected their poor pastor to meet all of those needs.

Today's passage shines its light upon our "needs" and shows us how these needs are *truly* met. In the end, these God-breathed words will point us away from concentrating on ourselves and being consumed by our needs and toward meeting the needs of others. Follow along with Paul's reasoning:

Philippians 2:1-4

¹ Therefore if there is any consolation in Christ, if any comfort of love, if any fellowship of the Spirit, if any affection and mercy,

² fulfill my joy by being like-minded, having the same love, being of one accord, of one mind.

³ Let nothing be done through selfish ambition or conceit, but in lowliness of mind let each esteem others better than himself.

⁴ Let each of you look out not only for his own interests, but also for the interests of others.

Out of God's Word...

1. In verse 1 Paul uses four phrases to point out the provisions given to each and every Christian. What are they?

   a.

   b.

   c.

   d.

2. Responsibility always comes with privilege. What does Paul say are the four responsibilities of each and every Christian (verse 2)?

   a.

   b.

   c.

   d.

3. Paul gives two admonitions, stated in the negative and in the positive (verses 3,4). Complete this chart:

	Do Not...	But	Do...
(Verse 3)			
(Verse 4)			

...and into your heart

• By the time my daughter Courtney told me she was memorizing the book of Philippians, she was already beginning Chapter 2—these very verses we're looking at here. I remember sharing with her that verse 1 means (and could read), "Therefore if there is any consolation in Christ [and of course there is!], if any comfort of love [and of course there is!], if any fellowship of the Spirit [and of course there is!], if any affection and mercy [and of course there is!]...."

It's true. Paul is conveying here that every Christian has been given consolation in Christ, comfort of love, the fellowship of the Spirit, and God's affection and mercy. Therefore, we can be encouraged and comforted and know we are loved...at all times and in all places!

How do these truths minister to you in your circumstances and your needs?

- In verse 3 Paul tells us how the Philippians (and we) can be "of one accord, of one mind" (verse 2): He says it is by "lowliness of mind." Humility, then, is a key to peaceful relationships with others and peaceful unity in the church. A "low mind" is distinctively a Christian grace, and harmony and unity cannot be achieved without it.

Can you think of one way to set about nurturing lowliness of mind?

Heart Response

When I think of lowliness of mind, I can't help but think of flowers. They are beautiful, lovely, and sweet; and the more mature they are and the bigger their blossoms, the more their heads bow. And we also enjoy and benefit from the delightful perfumes made from their crushed blossoms. What inspiring pictures of humility! While we may desire the rare and exquisite grace of humility, how, we wonder, is such beauty realized? How can we nurture a heart of humility? Here are a few and mind time-honored, foolproof scriptural guidelines.

❧ *Know thyself.* Yes, we are made in the image of God (Genesis 1:27), but we are also sinners (Romans 3:10,23) in need of a renewed mind so as to *think* properly about ourselves (Romans 12:1-3).

❧ *Respect others.* Jesus told His disciples to major on service to others (Matthew 20:20-28). And He Himself (as we'll see in our next lesson) "did not come to be served, but to serve, and to give His life a ransom for many" (Mark 10:45). Indeed, as Paul exhorts, we are to consider others to be better than ourselves!

❧ *Pray faithfully.* Everything about prayer is humbling—from its posture to its petitions. It is in prayer that we bow ourselves humbly before God Almighty, confess our sins before a holy God, thank and praise our heavenly Father for all He has done for us, and entreat His mercy and omnipotence on behalf of others. Prayer is humble dependence on God (1 Peter 5:6-7). Oh, please pray faithfully!

❧ *Imitate Christ's humility.* Peeking ahead, read Philippians 2:5-11. This, dear one, is *the key* to lowliness of mind.

In light of these sacred thoughts from Philippians 2:1-4, what the gifted English preacher Charles Haddon Spurgeon said about humility makes perfect sense: "Humility is the proper estimate of oneself."

Lesson 9

Living Like Jesus

*A*s we contemplate these next powerful words from Paul it's helpful to realize there were two problems in the Philippian church. Problem #1 (as we'll see later) was false teachers imparting false doctrine. Problem #2 was a lack of unity in the church caused by internal factions. As we saw in our last lesson, Paul spoke to the issue of unity, exhorting the Philippians (and us!) to walk humbly and to regard others as better than ourselves; to look out, not for ourselves only, but also for others.

Imagine the readers of this letter perhaps pausing, looking up from the papyrus and at one another, wondering, "But *how* does one achieve this prescribed humility and lowliness of mind?!"

It seems like Paul anticipated this question. Aren't you glad he proceeded to answer it? And *what an answer!* Realize that you stand on holy ground as Paul delivers the ultimate lesson on humility. Read...and savor it...now.

Philippians 2:5-11

⁵ Let this mind be in you which was also in Christ Jesus,

⁶ who, being in the form of God, did not consider it robbery to be equal with God,

⁷ but made Himself of no reputation, taking the form of a servant, and coming in the likeness of men.

⁸ And being found in appearance as a man, he humbled Himself and became obedient to the point of death, even the death of the cross.

⁹ Therefore God also has highly exalted Him and given Him the name which is above every name,

¹⁰ that at the name of Jesus every knee should bow, of those in heaven, and of those on earth, and of those under the earth,

¹¹ and that every tongue should confess that Jesus Christ is Lord, to the glory of God the Father.

Out of God's Word...

1. With what command does Paul begin this passage of Scripture (verse 5)?

2. It's been said that if we wish to follow in the steps of Jesus, we must remember that the way up is down. Can

you pick out several of the steps "downward" that Jesus in His humility took (verses 6-8)? Jot them here, and pause to contemplate one man's comments on these verses.

> *V*erses 6-8 form a very short passage: but there is no passage in the New Testament which so movingly sets out the utter reality of the godhead and the manhood of Jesus and makes so vivid the sacrifice that he made when he laid aside his godhead and took manhood upon him. How it happened, we cannot tell, but it is the mystery of a love so great that, although we can never fully understand it, we can blessedly experience it and adore it."[11]
>
> — William Barclay

3. What was the result, on a human level, of Jesus' humiliation (verse 8)?

And what was the result on a divine level (verse 9)?

...and into your heart

• Dying to self is indeed hard! Our inherent sin nature causes us to be selfish, grasping, ambitious, fleshly people. And yet the example we have in our dear Lord Jesus is one of complete selflessness and sacrifice for others. Can you think of something you may be holding on to or grasping or striving to attain that does not fit with Jesus' exquisite example of selflessness?

Can you think of some ways you can be more of a servant to others?

Heart Response

Do you wonder how so few verses (seven!) can contain such riches? There is so much to think about and to contemplate! As I reflect on the awfulness (Jesus' death) and awesomeness (Jesus' exaltation) of these truths, my mind runs towards theses thoughts and responses:

Walk. As Paul exhorts, "Let this mind be in you which was also in Christ Jesus." This is a call to obedience, fellow follower of the Lord. We must follow in Jesus' steps and choose to tread the pathway of lowly obedience. How?

—By willfully refusing to hold on to any perceived rights and privileges.

—By willfully laying aside these rights and privileges.

—By willfully taking on the nature of a servant.

—By willfully abasing and humbling ourselves.

—By willfully obeying God even if that obedience could mean death.

Witness. If, in time, every knee will bow and every tongue will confess that Jesus Christ is Lord, we must begin to tell others now!

Worship. I can never read these verses detailing Christ's humility—and humiliation in death—and exaltation as Lord "above all" without pausing to worship. Let's pause together and...

...thank our God for His Son, who emptied Himself and died on a cross for us.

...thank Him, too, for His Son's example of perfect humility.

...thank Him for the glorious exaltation of Jesus.

...fall on our knees now and confess Jesus as Lord and exalt Him personally.

Living Like Paul

Philippians 2:12-18

arenting is an assignment from God that is always accompanied by a multitude of hopes and dreams and prayers. With a heart overflowing with love for your dear children, you bear down during the formative years to ensure that truth, values, training, and discipline are applied in ample measure. Prayers are lifted moment by moment, day by day, year by year, for the ultimate outcome of your love and labors—will they, you wonder, grow up...to love the Lord?...to follow in God's ways?...to heed the Word of the Lord?...to be conformed to the image of Christ?...to point others to the Savior?

As we step into these practical verses from the mind of God, it helps to realize that Paul is giving a parental lesson here. He's already laid the groundwork in the lives of the readers, his "beloved" children at Philippi, in time past. And now that he's separated from them, he asks that they be sure to fulfill in their lives the spiritual accomplishments that make evident their faith in their Savior. Oh, how he yearns for fruit in their lives!

Pay close attention as he exhorts his spiritual children.

Philippians 2:12-18

12 Therefore, my beloved, as you have always obeyed, not as in my presence only, but now much more in my absence, work out your own salvation with fear and trembling;

13 for it is God who works in you both to will and to do for His good pleasure.

14 Do all things without murmuring and disputing,

15 that you may become blameless and harmless, children of God without fault in the midst of a crooked and perverse generation, among whom you shine as lights in the world,

16 holding fast the word of life, so that I may rejoice in the day of Christ that I have not run in vain or labored in vain.

17 Yes, and if I am being poured out as a drink offering on the sacrifice and service of your faith, I am glad and rejoice with you all.

18 For the same reason you also be glad and rejoice with me.

Out of God's Word...

This passage has been disputed for centuries, but for this part of our lesson, please copy the Bible text "out of God's Word" for your answers.

1. The Philippians had always done what Paul asked of them when he was with them; now, in his absence, he asks them for the same faithful obedience. Exactly what is he asking them to do (verse 12)?

   And *why* is he asking it (verse 13)?

   And *how* does he ask them to do it (verse 14)?

2. Paul also had a reason for what he asked of the Philippians—a *why:* He wanted them to "shine as lights in the world" as an obvious contrast to the darkness of evil (verses 15-16). Fill in this chart with the obvious contrasts.

Children of God	Children of the World
1. (verse 15)	1. (verse 15)
2. (verse 15)	2. (verse 15)
3. (verse 15)	
4. (verse 16)	

3. Next Paul moves to his personal suffering. What is his attitude toward it (verse 17)?

   What attitude did he want his friends to have regarding his suffering (verse 18)?

...and into your heart

- Perhaps the folks in Philippi were too reliant on Paul's presence and guidance. Now that Paul is away from them, he sets about reminding them who it is they really serve...and why: "For it is *God* who works in you both to will and to do for *His* good pleasure" (verse 13, emphasis added). Their assignment from God—not from Paul—was to work out their salvation—to carry it to its conclusion and apply it to day-by-day living. Their responsibility was to actively pursue obedience (verse 12). God's responsibility was to produce the spiritual fruit in their lives (verse 13) as they yielded to Him.

  And you, dear one? First, ask yourself if there is any one person—or group of persons—you may be relying upon to encourage you in your spiritual walk and work. Thank God for good Christian friends...and thank them, too!

  And second, remember the words of Jesus, who said, "I am the vine, you are the branches. He who abides in Me, and I in him, bears much fruit; for without Me you can do nothing" (John 15:5). Thank God for His Holy Spirit and His fruit in your life.

  And third, determine to actively obey the Lord in your daily life. Are you actively pursuing obedience? How can you do that today?

- A good teacher always anticipates his students' questions, and Paul is an outstanding teacher! As he pointed his Philippian friends to The Supreme Example of humility and sacrifice—our dear Lord's death (2:5-11)—he perhaps imagined their objection to the example: "Yes, but...that's Jesus! Surely you don't expect us to behave like Him! Why, Jesus was perfect!"

If that is what the readers of the epistle of Philippians were thinking (and you, too, dear friend?), Paul puts their objections to rest by pointing to the "sacrifice and service" of *their* faith...upon which he is pouring out his life as a sacrifice. Like an oblation of wine (the "drink offering" of the Old Testament—verse 17), Paul is pouring out his life on the altar of sacrifice. The picture here is of the flaming glory produced when the wine offering hits the fire of the altar of sacrifice.

Heart Response

I mentioned Dr. Louis Talbot earlier, and also his wife, Dr. Carol Talbot. After her husband's death, Carol Talbot wrote a biography of Louis's life and entitled it *For This I Was Born!* I loved reading about the fascinating and inspiring life of this great saint, preacher, and founder of a Bible institute and seminary; but I especially love the title. How wonderful to be able to know and to say, "For this I was born!"

Do you know what your purpose is, dear one? Can you boldly declare, "For this I was born!" and know what the "this" is? Knowing what the "this" is in my life is an issue I pray about each and every day—to know who I am in Christ and what I am called by Him to do (and to sacrifice!) for Him and His people. Jesus clearly stated, "For this cause I was born!" (John 18:37). And Paul, here in Philippians 2:17-18, is showing us what a life of purpose and sacrifice looks like. Are you living out your purpose for God's good pleasure, willing to sacrifice yourself, without murmuring and disputing?

esson 11

Living Like Timothy

ave you ever said "Yes, but…"? It's amazing how two tiny words can send such a strong signal of a lack of faith or understanding. In our last lesson, we imagined that perhaps the Philippians were pondering Jesus' example of sacrifice on behalf of others and saying, "Yes, but…that's *Jesus!*" We saw how Paul pointed out that *he* was "being poured out as a drink offering on the sacrifice and service of [their] faith" (verse 17). In other words, *both* he *and* the Philippians were offering their lives sacrificially and faithfully.

Next Paul proceeds to give a third example of sacrificial service. Moving to his assistant and traveling companion Timothy, Paul seems to say, "OK. Here's another person who thinks of others and not of himself."

As you read Paul's description of Timothy, keep in mind these facts about Timothy. He was:

—the son of a Greek father, who was not a believer in Christ (Acts 16:3)

—the son of a Jewish mother, Eunice, and the grandson of Lois (2 Timothy 2:5)

—Paul's child in the Lord (1 Corinthians 4:17)

—Paul's companion in prison in Rome (Philippians 1:1)

—Paul's assistant in the writing of at least five of his letters

Philippians 2:19-24

19 But I trust in the Lord Jesus to send Timothy to you shortly, that I also may be encouraged when I know your state.

20 For I have no man like-minded, who will sincerely care for your state.

21 For all seek their own, not the things which are of Christ Jesus.

22 But you know his proven character, that as a son with his father he served with me in the gospel.

23 Therefore I hope to send him at once, as soon as I see how it goes with me.

24 But I trust in the Lord that I myself shall also come shortly.

Out of God's Word...

1. After reading these wonderful verses, describe Timothy's relationship with Paul.

2. In your own words, note some of Timothy's character qualities.

3. How did Timothy differ from some others Paul knew (verse 21)?

...*and into your heart*

- Read again Philippians 2:5-8. How does Timothy exhibit the attitude and mind of Christ?

- Describe the importance of humility when ministering to others.

- And you, dear friend? What one behavior, heart concern, loyalty, or "sacrifice" drawn from the example of Timothy can you take away with you today and begin to weave into your own life of humble service to God's people?

Heart Response

The spectacular portrait of Timothy in this passage of Scripture causes conviction to flood my soul. How, dear friend, can you and I live more like Timothy?

⁣ *First—Submit yourself to God.* You are His servant.

⁣ *Second—Submit yourself to another.* Perhaps to become a Timothy we need to first submit ourselves to a Paul. Timothy served *with* Paul in the gospel. Do you have someone you serve with shoulder to shoulder? Is there an older woman or another woman you help as she serves the Lord?

⁣ *Third—Mature in usefulness.* Beloved, we need to sharpen our ministry skills and attitudes. We need to strengthen our faith. We need to increase our knowledge of the sacred Scriptures. As we spend T-I-M-E with a mentor and in ministry and in prayer and in Bible study, we mature in usefulness. (And remember that, at the time of the writing of Philippians, Timothy had been on Paul's ministry team for over ten years!)

⁣ *Fourth—Be content to play "second fiddle."* Harmony is produced in ministry when everyone seeks to be a servant.

During an interview with famed orchestra conductor Leonard Bernstein, the interviewer asked, "Mr. Bernstein, what is the most difficult instrument to play?" With quick wit, Bernstein responded, "Second fiddle." He said, "I can get plenty of first violinists but to find one who plays second violin with as much enthusiasm, or second French horn or second flute, now that's a problem. And yet," he added, "if no one plays second, we have no harmony."[12]

☙ *Fifth—Commit to "The Four A's."* Could you sign the statement below, which was once given to a group of conference attendees?

For You, Lord...   **A**ny thing
                    Any where
                    Any time
                    At any cost

_____

Sign here

Timothy was an amazing saint and an amazing servant. He was invaluable and irreplaceable because his one desire was to serve Paul and Jesus Christ. He was quite content with the second place, so long as he could serve the Lord. May God make each of us more like Timothy!

Living Like Epaphroditus

*H*ave you ever heard an important person—perhaps a guest speaker or a new officer—introduced? The remarks are usually delivered in glowing language. Well, today's assignment introduces us to yet another person who emulated Jesus in sacrificial service. Paul has already pointed us to the supreme example of Jesus' sacrifice for us. Then Paul, writing from a cell, reported that he was pouring out his life as a sacrifice on top of the sacrifice of the Philippians. Next Paul commended Timothy, his "twin" in the faith, the man whom Paul considered to be likeminded with him. Yes, Timothy sincerely cared for the Philippians and, unlike others who were concerned only about themselves, would make every sacrifice for those in the church at Philippi.

Perhaps...it's possible...just one more time...the Philippian readers uttered those two awful words again—"Yes, but..." and then added, "...that's Timothy! He gets to walk with you, Paul, and talk with you. Just count his many blessings and privileges!" Well, dear one, if this were the case, Paul was up to the challenge. He had one final person for his friends in Philippi to look to for the Christlike behavior of servanthood, and that was a man just like them—Epaphroditus. In fact, Epaphroditus was from their own congregation.

Note the lovely language used by Paul to describe Epaphroditus, whose name means *lovely*, and oh, what a lovely person he was!

Philippians 2:25-30

25 Yet I considered it necessary to send to you Epaphroditus, my brother, fellow worker, and fellow soldier, but your messenger and the one who ministered to my need;

26 since he was longing for you all, and was distressed because you had heard that he was sick.

27 For indeed he was sick almost unto death; but God had mercy on him, and not only on him but on me also, lest I should have sorrow upon sorrow.

28 Therefore I sent him the more eagerly, that when you see him again you may rejoice, and I may be less sorrowful.

29 Receive him therefore in the Lord with all gladness, and hold such men in esteem;

30 because for the work of Christ he came close to death, not regarding his life, to supply what was lacking in your service toward me.

Out of God's Word...

1. How does Paul describe Epaphroditus in relation to...
   himself (verses 25,30)?

   the Philippians (verses 25, 30)?

2. What had been Ephaproditus's physical condition (verses
   26-27), and what had made the difference (verse 27)?

3. What two purposes would sending Epaphroditus accomplish (verse 28)?

4. What role in Paul's life had Epaphroditus played on
   behalf of the Philippians (verse 30)?

...and into your heart

- Read again Philippians 2:5-8. How does Epaphroditus
  exhibit the attitude and mind of Christ?

- Can you follow the "circle of love" drawn in this passage of Scripture?

The Philippians cared for Paul, so ...
The Philippians sent Epaphroditus to assist him.
Epaphroditus, in the course of ministry to Paul,
    became sick unto death.
The Philippians heard about his illness and became
    worried about Epaphroditus.
Epaphroditus then worried about the Philippians' concerns for him.
Paul cared for the Philippians and Epaphroditus so
    much that ...
Paul sent Epaphroditus back to the Philippians.

Do you sense the loving care displayed here? That's the way it should be in the body of Christ. No matter who we are or what our position, we are called to care, to love, to give, to minister, and to sacrifice. And in that way, everyone benefits!

You see, this "circle of love" was lived out *through* people and to people. The Philippians couldn't go to Paul—but they could send Epaphroditus to him. And Paul couldn't go to the Philippians—but he could send Timothy and Epaphroditus to them. Each of these men was living out the presence and reality of Christ in their lives. Each was living out the admonition of Philippians 2:5, to "let this mind be in you which was also in Christ Jesus." Are you involved in God's "circle of love" when it comes to those closest to you? What can you do today to follow in the steps of Paul, Timothy, and Epaphroditus as you serve others?

- Do you consider yourself to be one of these "lovely" servants of the Lord? Our service may never be performed on the platforms upon which these "stars" let their lights shine for Jesus (2:15). But you, too, are surrounded by people who need your selfless, Christlike service. Do you perhaps have a husband, young children, married children, grandchildren, parents or in-laws, co-workers, neighbors, and friends who need the loving, sacrificial touch of a Jesus, a Paul, a Timothy, and an Epaphroditus? Why not follow in the steps of our dear Lord and these three faithful disciples? Take on the role of a servant, empty yourself of yourself, humble yourself (2:7-8), and reach out and touch those in your path. "Let this mind be in you which was also in Christ Jesus" (2:5)! Jot down how you will begin.

Heart Response

I have to admit that I've had the "Yes, but…" thought about this passage myself. But my "Yes, but…" question runs like this: "Yes, but…Paul and Timothy and Epaphroditus were *men!* Is there an example of a *woman* that I might look to?"

Thank the Lord that His Word is filled to overflowing with women who set examples of selfless service! Just think of Esther, the Shunuamite woman, Priscilla, and Dorcas. (Indeed, such noble women mean so much to me that I've even written a book detailing the sacrifices of more than a hundred of these wonderful women of faith.)

However, on a more contemporary note, meet Amy Carmichael. A single woman and a missionary to India in the late 1800s and early 1900s, this dear lady did not take a break from her mission service for 55 years. No, as the woman who wrote this prayer,

> Let me not think to be a clod.
> Make me Thy fuel, flame of God,

Amy Carmichael poured out her life for the gospel's sake and for the sake of others. The organization she founded, The Dohnavur Fellowship, provided homes for the young girls and boys she rescued from lives of servitude and shame in Hindu temples.

We too, dear sister, are called to selflessly serve those in our own God-ordained arenas. May you and I find the joy Paul spoke of in verse 17, when he said, "I am glad"; or, as the King James Version of the Bible exults, "If I be offered upon the sacrifice and service of your faith, I joy, and rejoice with you all."

Warning the Flock

Philippians 3:1-3

*H*ow do you respond when you see a sign or hear an announcement with this one word only: "WARNING!"? How we acknowledge and react to a warning has far-reaching effects. Indeed, it can save our life! I once read of a missionary father serving in an African jungle who spotted his little son playing under a tree, a tree with a giant boa constrictor snake hanging out of it over his little boy! His love and concern yelled out the warning that would save the tot's life…only if he obeyed.

Well, dear friend, Paul begins Philippians 3 with a warning. You see, he loves his friends there in Philippi. And, because of that love, he has their good in mind. As Paul thinks about certain issues in the church and problems that are plaguing the church there, he as much as yells "WARNING!" And, as with the young boy, the Christians at Philippi would be safe...only if they obeyed.

It's a brief warning, but give heed as you read it. Your own well-being may depend on it!

Philippians 3:1-3

¹ Finally, my brethren, rejoice in the Lord. For me to write the same things to you is not tedious, but for you it is safe.

² Beware of dogs, beware of evil workers, beware of the mutilation!

³ For we are the circumcision, who worship God in the Spirit, rejoice in Christ Jesus, and have no confidence in the flesh...

Out of God's Word...

1. What wonderful reminder does Paul give the Philippians (and us!) in verse 1?

As Paul prepares to repeat something, what reason does he give for the repetition (verse 1)?

2. List the 3 warnings Paul gives to his friends (verse 2).

a.

b.

c.

3. What are the three components of "the true circumcision"
as described by Paul (verse 3)?

a.

b.

c.

...*and into your heart*

- In these verses Paul appears to be warning against
  Judaizing teachers. These teachers were attempting to put
  the church back under the rigid regulations of the Mosaic
  law and the traditions of the Jews. In other words, Christians whose salvation was by the grace of Jesus Christ
  were being re-harnessed by these teachers with the
  legalism and rules contained in the Old Testament Law,
  which was handed down by God to Moses in the book
  of Exodus.

  Even though Paul wrote these words of warning almost
  2,000 years ago, there is still a tendency to put man-made
  "rules" and "works" into our lives that are not necessary
  for New Testament Christians who have been saved by
  God's grace. What are the "laws" and "works" God is
  interested in?

  Matthew 22:36-40—

  John 13:34—

  Romans 13:8-10—

Galatians 5:22-23—

James 2:8—

- As points of information: "Dogs" was a designation used by Jews in referring to Gentiles. This term carried with it the idea of being impure and unclean. For instance, dogs in the ancient world were scavengers feeding on garbage and filth, fighting among themselves and attacking those who passed by. The thought is that these Judaizing teachers, like dogs, were eating the garbage (i.e., man-made rules and works) from the table instead of seeking to live a life of obedience sitting down at the banquet table of the grace of God.

  "Evil workers" were those guilty of evil deeds. There's great irony in this term: The Jews, because they kept the Mosaic law, considered themselves to be workers of righteousness. And yet, as they taught those who were free from the law in Christ that they, too, must keep the law to be saved, they became workers of evil.

  "Mutilation" is a reference to the law of the circumcision of the flesh as laid down in the Old Testament Law. However, as Christians, our hearts have been circumcised (Romans 2:29; Colossians 2:11)!

- Paul points out that true believers in Jesus Christ—those saved by and whose works flow *from* their salvation—are those of us who worship God in the Spirit, rejoice in Christ Jesus, and have no confidence in the flesh.

  ...we worship God in the Spirit: Our spiritual life is empowered by the Holy Spirit.

  ...we rejoice in Jesus rather than glory in our own works.

...we have no confidence in the flesh, but joy in the grace of Christ.

I know this is a lot to ponder and understand. The essence is this, beloved: The basis of our union with Christ is never the works that we do, but the work that Jesus did...on the cross! As Ephesians 2:8-9 declares, "For by grace you have been saved through faith, and that not of yourselves; it is the gift of God, not of works, lest anyone should boast."

Heart Response

Details and definitions! They tend to boggle the mind, don't they? Let us simply grasp the two clear truths in these few verses of warning.

First, we must obey God's Word, not man-made religious rules and regulations. We must seek to live our lives *God's* way, to walk in a manner worthy of our calling in Him.

Second, we must put no confidence in the flesh. There is nothing we can ever do to earn or enhance our status with our dear Lord. He, in His gracious love, has secured our sonship for us. Hallelujah, what a Savior!

This lesson, dear one, calls us to worship. And that's exactly what a woman just like you and me did one Sunday morning back in 1865. As Elvina Hall sat in the choir loft of the Monument Street Methodist Church of Baltimore, her pastor's sermon moved her to grab her hymnal and jot down on the flyleaf of the book the words running through her heart. Her worship became a song many churches still sing today at communion, "Jesus Paid It All." As the chorus to this anthem of our faith so eloquently proclaims:

Jesus paid it all.
All to Him I owe;
Sin had left a crimson stain,
He washed it white as snow.

Prayer to pray:

Father, thank You for the provision You have made for my salvation through Christ. It is all of Thee, and none of me. May I worship in the Spirit of God, glory in Your Son, Jesus Christ, and put no confidence in the flesh! Amen.

Losing All to Gain All

Philippians 3:4-7

The apostle Paul was truly an amazing person! While it's one thing to glean insights about him from the Bible and from history and reference books, it's quite another to hear it from his own mouth. As you may know, Paul referred to himself as "less than the least of all the saints" (Ephesians 3:8). He said, "I am the least of the apostles, who am not worthy to be called an apostle" (1 Corinthians 15:9). And, when pointing to Jesus' saving of sinners, Paul added, "of whom I am chief" (1 Timothy 1:15).

Yes, Paul was powerful. (Indeed, as a teacher and preacher, he was called "Mercurius" or "Hermes" after the herald of the Greek gods, because he was such a forceful speaker.) But on the occasion of writing to his friends in

Philippi, he tells us about his background and privileges, a little about his upbringing—his pedigree, if you will.

As you read these few concise, to-the-point verses, remember that Paul has just warned his readers to "have *no* confidence in the flesh" (3:3). Then, in this passage of Scripture, he details some of the blessings in his own life that *could* have given him cause for "confidence in the flesh." Enjoy learning about the life of Paul in his own words...but don't miss how he ends his message!

Philippians 3:4-7

4 ...though I also might have confidence in the flesh. If anyone else thinks he may have confidence in the flesh, I more so:

5 circumcised the eighth day, of the stock of Israel, of the tribe of Benjamin, a Hebrew of the Hebrews; concerning the law, a Pharisee;

6 concerning zeal, persecuting the church; concerning the righteousness which is in the law, blameless.

7 But what things were gain to me, these I have counted loss for Christ.

Out of God's Word...

1. Paul first points to four advantages he enjoyed from birth. Find them in verse 5 and list them here.

   a.

   b.

   c.

   d.

Next, Paul names three personal achievements in the Jewish faith in which he could boast (verses 5-6).

a.

b.

c.

2. Yes, Paul could have bragged, boasted, and counted on his heredity and zeal for personal righteousness...but how did he view his privileges and achievements as compared to righteousness by faith in Christ (verse 7)? Write out verse 7 here.

...*and into your heart*

- Paul certainly had many advantages from birth, as well as many notable achievements. And so do you! Can you jot a few of them here? Don't forget to thank God for each and every one of them!

- But Paul knew the superiority of trusting in Jesus Christ for salvation, of having that righteousness "which is through faith in Christ" (Philippians 3:9), instead of his personal blessings and attainments. How do you view your personal privileges and successes when laid next to the surpassing worth of knowing Jesus? Can you say along with Paul, "What things were gain to me, these I have counted loss for Christ"?

Heart Response

I thank God that He's given us these glimpses into Paul's passion for Christ. Paul was a man with one desire—to have no other concern in His life but Jesus. He thought nothing of giving up all and living his life for the One who saved him. Because Jesus Christ had achieved righteousness for him, Paul counted everything else in his life a loss. For Paul the "gain" of the grace of God was greater than any "gain" in his personal life.

Yes, I thank God for the example of Paul. And I also thank the Lord for the example of C. T. Studd, a missionary who died in 1931. Take to heart these details of the life of a man who had incredible wealth and advantage, yet counted it all loss for the priceless privilege of knowing Christ.

At the age of 16 C. T. Studd was already an expert cricket player and at 19 was made captain of his team at Eton, England. Soon he became a world-famous sports personality. But the Lord had different plans for him, for while attending Cambridge University he heard D. L. Moody preach and was wondrously converted. He soon dedicated his life and his inherited wealth to Christ and spent hours seeking to convert his teammates. Sensing God's leading to full-time service, he offered himself to Hudson Taylor for missionary work in China.

While in that foreign country, C. T. Studd inherited a sum of money equivalent today to half a million dollars. In 24 hours he gave the entire inheritance away, investing it in the things of the Lord. Later he was forced to go back to England, for his health was failing and his wife was an invalid. But God called him again—this time to the heart of Africa. He was informed that if he went, he would not live long. His only answer was that he had been looking for a chance to die for Jesus' "faithful unto death." He accepted God's call and labored until the Savior took him Home.[14]

—Paul Lee Tan

How is your bookkeeping, dear one? Paul—and C. T. Studd—could have kept a ledger sheet of losses and gains. It's thrilling (and challenging) to see how these two wonderful converts to Christ gave up all to follow Jesus. All their inherent advantages and privileges, along with all their outstanding feats, swept away, believing "what things were gain to me, these I have counted loss for Christ."

How does your ledger sheet look, my friend? I'm praying for both of us—that we will put no confidence in the flesh to merit or earn salvation but glory rather in all that Jesus has done *for* us and has given *to* us! As the piercing words of Isaac Watts' revered old hymn *When I Survey the Wondrous Cross* declare,

When I survey the wondrous cross
On which the Prince of glory died,
My richest gain I count but loss,
And pour contempt on all my pride.

Lesson 15

Knowing God

*H*ave you ever taken a spiritual inventory, my friend? I remember hearing a young man tell about one of the blessings that came out of an awful automobile accident that resulted in the amputation of one of his legs. Can you imagine *any* blessings coming from such a trauma?! As this man explained, his months in a hospital bed gave him the opportunity to evaluate his spiritual life—to take a spiritual inventory. You see, as an active young adult he had just been too busy to pay much attention to his spiritual life. But that downtime prodded this gentleman to spend time alone with God to look at his life.

Well, in today's passage God's servant Paul gives us the results of his own personal spiritual inventory. In clear terms, he relates to us the reassessment of his spiritual life after his conversion. We already know that he counted loss for Christ all the things that were previously counted as gain. His upbringing and religious training were thrown aside, along with his privileged education and religious zeal. And in his new evaluation of these "things" and "all things," Paul rejects them with horror and treats them as liabilities.

Read along and learn, as Paul has, what is truly important when it comes to taking inventory of the "things" in our life.

Philippians 3:8-11

⁸ But indeed I also count all things loss for the excellence of the knowledge of Christ Jesus my Lord, for whom I have suffered the loss of all things, and count them as rubbish, that I may gain Christ

⁹ and be found in Him, not having my own righteousness, which is from the law, but that which is through faith in Christ, the righteousness which is from God by faith;

¹⁰ that I may know Him and the power of His resurrection, and the fellowship of His sufferings, being conformed to His death,

¹¹ if, by any means, I may attain to the resurrection from the dead.

Out of God's Word...

1. Reread verse 7 from our previous lesson, where Paul referred to some of the "things" that were "gain" to him. But now in verse 8, what inclusive adjective does Paul use twice?

What makes "all things" pale and fade in importance (verse 8)?

After Paul counts all things as loss, what final label does he put on all fleshly assets (verse 8)?

And what does Paul desire to gain instead (verse 8)?

2. List the desires of Paul's heart:

   a. Verse 9—That I may

   b. Verse 10—That I may

   c. Verse 10—That I may

   d. Verse 10—That I may

   e. Verse 10—That I may

   f. Verse 11—That I may

...and into your heart

• Can you think of ways you can begin to value "things" less and Christ more? Note several here.

• Considering Paul's heart-cry in verse 10, how do you think you can know Jesus better? (Remember, the emphasis here is on gaining a deeper knowledge and intimacy with Christ.)

• Set up an appointment on your personal calendar to spend time taking your own spiritual inventory. (And be sure you take this sacred passage of Scripture along with you for your appointment!)

Heart Response

Beloved, I want to know my Savior. It's one of the consuming passions of my life (and of yours, I hope!). And I want to know Him better and better with each passing day. True, knowing Jesus is believing in Him. But knowing Jesus is also experiential, progressive knowledge. As you and I learn more about Him from the Bible and learn more about Him through drawing upon His resurrection power over sin and death, believe me, we're fulfilling that passion to know Him!

But what does "being conformed to His death" mean? We begin the process by putting sin aside (Ephesians 4:22). Why? Because we are conformed to Christ's death when we die to sin (Romans 6:10-11), when we are crucified with Christ (Galatians 2:20), when the flesh and its affections are put to death (Colossians 3:5), and when the world is crucified to us (Galatians 6:14). This, my friend, is how we are conformed to Jesus' death.

Does it sound like a lot to accomplish? Well, take to heart these words spoken by C. T. Studd (whose life we looked at in the previous lesson): "If Jesus be God and died for me, then no sacrifice can be too great for me to make for Him."

Lesson 16

Conquering by Continuing

I'm sure you've had people ask you to share your favorite Bible verse with them. People frequently ask me to do that, and it's always hard to respond. I guess I have to say that I have multiple favorite verses. But there's no doubt that one of those favorites is 2 Corinthians 5:17: "Therefore, if anyone is in Christ, he is a new creation; old things have passed away; behold, all things have become new." It's just so comforting to know that in salvation our past sins and failures have been wiped away by the grace of God!

How thrilling it is to know that, according to the Bible, as Christians we are new creatures or creations in Christ! And while that was certainly true of the apostle Paul, he did not want to give the impression that he had arrived at spiritual perfection. So, as we step into today's passage of Scripture, we read that Paul (just like you and I) is still very much involved in the race of life. Read as he explains:

Philippians 3:12-14

[12] Not that I have already attained, or am already perfected; but I press on, that I may lay hold of that for which Christ Jesus has also laid hold of me.

[13] Brethren, I do not count myself to have apprehended; but one thing I do, forgetting those things which are behind and reaching forward to those things which are ahead,

[14] I press toward the goal for the prize of the upward call of God in Christ Jesus.

Out of God's Word...

1. What one accomplishment was Paul intent upon (verse 12)?

And what action was he taking to attain it (verse 12)?

2. Jesus Christ laid hold of, or grasped, Paul when he was on his way to Damascus (see Acts 9:1-19). After that encounter, Paul was possessed completely by Christ and desired only to lay hold of, or to grasp, the purpose for which he was grasped by Jesus. And so Paul is now pressing on in hot pursuit of the call Jesus made on his life. Paul likens his hot pursuit to a race in which he is a runner.

A runner has an aim. What words in verse 13 indicate Paul's focus?

3. But a runner also needs concentration. Note these stages of Paul's concentration:

Verse 13—Regarding the past,
Paul _____

Verse 13—Regarding progression,
Paul _____

Verse 14—Regarding the goal,
Paul _____

...and into your heart

- According to Paul's example, we should always concentrate our energies on moving forward now and continuing to move forward in the future. Where are you putting your focus?

- Are there "things" that hinder your forward focus? Can you name them and then determine how to "lay aside every weight, and the sin which so easily ensnares us, and...run with endurance the race that is set before us" (Hebrews 12:1)?

- What can you do today to

Forget those things that are behind?

Reach forward?

Press toward the goal?

Heart Response

"But one thing I do...." How would you finish this statement, dear friend? The famous preacher D. L. Moody wrote these words from a scholar named Gannett in the margin of his Bible beside Philippians 3:13: "Men may be divided into two classes—those who have a 'one thing' and those who have no 'one thing' to do; those with aim, and those without aim in their lives.... The aim in life is what the backbone is to the body: Without it we are invertebrate."

How frightening it would be to be "invertebrate"—to be spineless, weak, and weak willed—especially in the Christian life! But thanks be to God for these cherished-yet-instructive verses about the process whereby you and I may know and accomplish our "one thing"—attaining the great prize of the Christian race. What are the steps that make up the process?

- Mental obliteration. A runner never looks back, but mentally obliterates the part of the course which he has already covered.

- Unwavering progression. A runner strains every nerve and muscle as he keeps on running with all his might toward the goal. Indeed, his hand is stretched out as if to grasp it. He is thinking all along the way, "I want this win!"

- A goal in view. A runner's eyes are always fixed on the goal. And that goal is at the end of the race, not some other place through the course. Whether that goal was a pillar or a person, the sight of it and the contemplation of reward compelled the runner ever goal-ward.

Oh, beloved pursuer of God's prize, are you refusing to look back? Are you pressing and straining forward with unwavering progression? And are you ever looking to the prize of the upward call of God in Christ Jesus? In the words of the blind Scottish minister, George Matheson, "We conquer—not in any brilliant fashion—we conquer by continuing." May you and I conquer by continuing! Press on, dear one!

Maturing in Christ

Philippians 3:15-16

Every four years, athletes from around the globe gather to compete in the Olympic Games. Though the sporting events are varied, the athletes' goal is singular—to win gold, silver, and bronze medals for their countries. The world's fastest and best-trained runners never fail to enthrall us (and leave us breathless!) as they compete in the track and field events. As we watch the races, we take for granted the athletes' iron legs, reaching arms, straining muscles…and grimacing faces. They have trained—for years. And they have disciplined themselves—for years. There's no way these athletes could endure such grueling preparation and agonizing exertion unless they had a grand goal in mind.

And, dear friend, our focus and perseverance should be like that of Olympic athletes as we look to the end of our race and focus on finishing well. The entry fee for competing—Christ's death (paid for us)—and the glorious prize that awaits us at the end are too priceless to trivialize by losing momentum, dropping behind, or failing to finish. So Paul, ever the exhorter, has a few more words for us on how to stay in the race. Read on!

Philippians 3:15-16

¹⁵ Therefore let us, as many as are mature, have this mind; and if in anything you think otherwise, God will reveal even this to you.

¹⁶ Nevertheless, to the degree that we have already attained, let us walk by the same rule, let us be of the same mind.

Out of God's Word...

1. Write out the first admonition Paul gives to his readers (verse 15).

   Thinking back to our previous lesson, what is the "mind" Paul is referring to?

2. It's always wonderful to learn more about God and His character and how He works in our life. What do we learn about Him here (verse 15)?

3. Now write out Paul's second admonition to his readers (verse 16).

...and into your heart

- What words would you use to state Paul's admonition in verse 16?

  In the positive? Do...

  In the negative? Do not...

- What would you advise another Christian to do to press harder for Christian maturity?

  And are you putting that same advice to work in your own pursuit of the goal? If not, what changes do you need to make or how can you increase the discipline needed to reach the goal?

Heart Response

Just two verses, beloved! But, oh what a powerful message! You see, our daily life as Christians is all about maturing in Christ. Paul was already "mature"...and yet he desired to continue moving forward in spiritual growth, to keep on reaching forward and pressing on, to keep on keeping on.

If you've come this far in our study of Paul's impassioned letter to the Philippians, I know that you, too, desire to grow in Christ, to develop a deeper love relationship with Him, to mature in understanding and usefulness. And so, I leave us with these fine words written by an eminent Greek scholar regarding these two verses packed with wisdom:

Paul says [these] things about pressing on toward maturity:

He is *forgetting the things which are behind.* That is to say, he will never glory in any of his achievements or use them as an excuse for relaxation. In effect Paul is saying that the Christian must forget all that he has done and remember only what he has still to do. In the Christian life there is no room for a person who desires to rest upon his laurels.

He is also *reaching out for the things which are in front.* The word he uses for *reaching out* is very vivid and is used of a racer going hard for the tape. It describes him with eyes for nothing but the goal. It describes the man who is going flat out for the finish. So Paul says that in the Christian life we must forget every past achievement and remember only the goal which lies ahead.

Paul pens verse 15 to mean this: "Anyone who has come to be mature in the faith and knows what Christianity is must recognize the discipline and the effort and the agony of the Christian life." He may perhaps think differently, but, if he is an honest man, God will make it plain to him that he must never relax his effort or lower his standards but must press toward the goal until the end.

As Paul saw it, the Christian is the athlete of Christ.[16]

So press on, fellow athlete of Christ. "Let us not deviate from those principles that have brought us safely to our present state of Christian maturity. The condition for future [spiritual growth and maturity] is to walk according to present light."[17]

Lesson 18

Following Those
Who Follow the Lord

An unknown person has written these words of wisdom. "There are four classes of men:

1. He who knows not, and knows not he knows not—He is a fool; shun him.
2. He who knows not, and knows he knows not—He is simple; teach him.
3. He who knows, and knows not he knows—He is asleep; waken him.
4. He who knows, and knows he knows—He is wise; follow him."

God's wonderful servant Paul shares with us in this next passage of Scripture words of wisdom on who we are to shun and who we are to follow. Pay close attention as he sketches for us two pictures—one of those who are friends of the cross and another of those who are "the enemies of the cross."

Philippians 3:17-21

[17] Brethren, join in following my example, and note those who so walk, as you have us for a pattern.

[18] For many walk, of whom I have told you often, and now tell you even weeping, that they are the enemies of the cross of Christ:

[19] whose end is destruction, whose god is their belly, and whose glory is in their shame—who set their mind on earthly things.

[20] For our citizenship is in heaven, from which we also eagerly wait for the Savior, the Lord Jesus Christ,

[21] who will transform our lowly body that it may be conformed to His glorious body, according to the working by which He is able even to subdue all things to Himself.

Out of God's Word...

1. Paul begins by first instructing the Philippian believers to do two things (verse 17):

   a.

   b.

Who does Paul suggest the Philippians should imitate (verse 17)?

And why were they to follow the example of these people (verse 18)?

2. Paul, the ever-faithful teacher, next describes and warns his fellow believers against those he labels "the enemies of the cross of Christ" (verse 18). List the four facts about these "enemies" that so mark them (verse 19).

a.

b.

c.

d.

And how do we as true believers differ from this group (verses 17 and 20)?

3. Did you know that this passage of God's Word also tells us some marvelous truths and facts about our dear Lord and Savior Jesus Christ? Name as many as you can here (see verses 20-21).

...*and into your heart*

- Sobering words, aren't they? Paul is telling us that the cross of Christ should make a difference in our daily life. In a few brief words, where should we as Christians place our focus and outlook?

After jotting down your own thoughts, consider these words about "the friends" and "the enemies" of the cross, which are also quite sobering!

If the *friends* of the cross are those who show in their lives that they have caught the spirit of the cross, namely, that of *self-denial*...then surely the *enemies* of the cross are those who manifest the very opposite attitude, namely, that of *self-indulgence*. The *friends* of the cross do not love the world. In fact, the world is crucified to them, and they to the world, and this because they glory in the cross (Galatians 6:14). The *enemies* of the cross love the world and the things that are in the world (1 John 2:15). They set their minds on earthly things (Philippians 3:19).

- Paul spoke of looking to an example and patterning our lives after those who are faithfully and earnestly following Jesus Christ, those who are friends of the cross. Do you currently know Christians whom you watch and follow as they follow the pattern set by Jesus and Paul? You may want to name them here and thank God for them, praying for their continued strong Christian walk and example to you and to others. Also consider what you might do to follow their Christlike pattern more intently.

• Jesus' return and His glorification and perfection of His saints obviously meant a lot to Paul in his suffering. How do verses 20 and 21 encourage you in yours?

Heart Response

Dear follower of Christ, there are many messages for you and me in these few verses:

❧ *Be following.* How blessed you are if you were able to name someone in the exercise above, someone God has given you to follow, someone who is a true friend of the cross, someone who shows you how to follow in Christ's footsteps! If perhaps you are new to the faith, or new to your church, beseech God to lead you…quickly!…to someone who is looking to the Lord and following hard after Him (Psalm 63:8).

❧ *Be modeling.* While I hope you have someone to follow, I also hope and pray you'll take on the challenge of being one who models for others what it means to be a true follower of Jesus. I pray that you, too, will be able to say along with Paul, "Imitate me, just as I also imitate Christ" (1 Corinthians 11:1).

❦ *Be alert*. We have been warned so that we can recognize those who are "the enemies of the cross" of Christ. Paul wept when he warned his friends (and us!). Let us take heed!

❦ *Be encouraged*. As we've just contemplated, the friends of the cross are called to self-denial along with a lifestyle of reaching and pressing, of straining and enduring. But we're to be encouraged, too: We will see Jesus, the one we wait for from heaven, and we will be changed into the image of Him, transformed into a likeness of His glorious body. As Paul loved to say, "Rejoice!"

esson 19

Living in Unity

hhh! Paul is approaching a sensitive issue, and you and I can learn a lot if we pay attention to *how* Paul, the master motivator, handles it! Paul's letter to the Philippian church has been short and sweet. Other than several warnings about false teachers (3:1-3) and "the enemies of the cross" (3:17-21), there's been nothing but praise and encouragement throughout Paul's epistle. But now as Paul begins to wrap up his letter, he must address a problem that existed in the body of believers there in Philippi. Unfortunately, part of the problem was in the "women's ministry" where two women were quarreling and causing problems. Paul—and the Lord—desired peace among believers, and so he speaks to the matter of disharmony. Apparently the differences between these two women in the church were affecting the close spirit of fellowship and harmony that should characterize the people of God. Hear Paul's appeal to these two women he valued so highly.

Philippians 4:1-3

¹ Therefore, my beloved and longed-for brethren, my joy and crown, so stand fast in the Lord, beloved.

² I implore Euodia and I implore Syntyche to be of the same mind in the Lord.

³ And I urge you also, true companion, help these women who labored with me in the gospel, with Clement also, and the rest of my fellow workers, whose names are in the Book of Life.

Out of God's Word...

1. What words of affection does Paul use to begin his exhortation (verse 1)?

   And what is it that he asks of the Philippians (verse 1)?

2. Verse 1 is general. However, in verse 2 Paul points to specific people. Who are they?

   And what does he ask of them (verse 2)?

   What was their relationship to Paul (verse 3)?

   How had they helped the body of Christ in the past (verse 3)?

3. Next, Paul mentions a "true companion" (verse 3). Exactly what was it Paul asked of this person?

...*and into your heart*

• Even as Paul approaches a problem issue in the Philippian church, he uses affectionate language. How is such affection nurtured? (see Philippians 1:3-8).

• What is the pattern of your thoughts and prayers toward others—even toward troublemakers?

• Every person mentioned in verses 1-3 was to make his or her contribution to the cause of unity in the church. What contribution are you currently making in your church body...or need to make?

• To the two women involved in a feud, Paul exhorts, "Be of the same mind in the Lord" or "live in harmony" (verse 2 NASB). Taken to heart, how can this admonition help you in your relationships within the church? And just as a reminder, according to Philippians 2:5, what is the "mind" or "attitude" we seek?

Heart Response

We began this lesson eavesdropping on Paul as he handled a delicate situation in the Philippian church. Euodia and Syntyche, two of his friends and co-workers for the cause of Christ, were having their differences. And the rift between them was causing a rift in the church. So how did Paul handle the problem? There is much here for us to learn, dear one.

First, Paul spoke directly to the two ladies (and anyone else who may have been involved in strife), imploring them to settle their dispute and live in harmony. Wisely, Paul based his appeal on the cause of Christ and not on his own wishes. He asked that they be of the same mind *in the Lord*, that they keep the peace and live in love. Paul also wisely directed them to view the bigger picture: the Lord, the Lord's church, and the progress of the Lord's work. They were to put aside their differences for the grander cause of the common good of the church at Philippi and the body of Christ.

Second, Paul praised these two women. Paul recalls how they labored shoulder to shoulder with him for the cause of the gospel. He also reminds them (and everyone else) that they had served with Clement and the rest of the workers for Christ.

Finally, Paul called upon others in the church to help Euodia and Syntyche. He encouraged their involvement in helping to solve the problem. These women had helped others, and now others needed to help them.

Oh, beloved, pray! Pray that *you* may not be the cause of any disruptions in your church, that *you* may not be a part of hindering the work of the church for the cause of Christ! And pray to follow in Paul's wise footsteps if you must ever be a part of helping to solve a dispute between others.

Lesson 20

Overcoming Anxiety

Every woman makes "to-do" lists, those abbreviated lists of things that need to be done. These catalogs of tasks, phone calls, reminders, and plans keep us on track so we get more done and better manage the events of day-to-day life.

Today's lesson, dear one, brings us a "to-do" list from the mind and wisdom of God's choice servant Paul. And, because one of the recurring themes of the book of Philippians is peace, Paul's "to-do" list shows us how to enjoy the peace that is available to us as Christians. You see, Paul so greatly desired peace among Christians in the body of Christ that he exhorts each individual Christian to possess the personal peace God offers. Only then can there be peace in the church.

I'm sure you're saying a hearty "Amen!" to Paul's logic, so let's look at his "to-do" list for peace. Read...and reflect.

Philippians 4:4-7

⁴ Rejoice in the Lord always. Again I will say, rejoice!

⁵ Let your gentleness be known to all men. The Lord is at hand.

⁶ Be anxious for nothing, but in everything by prayer and supplication, with thanksgiving, let your requests be made known to God;

⁷ and the peace of God, which surpasses all understanding, will guard your hearts and minds through Christ Jesus.

Out of God's Word...

1. Looking at the verses from our last lesson and at those for this lesson, complete Paul's three commands to his friends in the Philippian church:

   Stand fast _____ (4:1).

   Be of the same mind _____ (verse 2).

   Rejoice_____ (verse 4).

   Can you tell where Paul's emphasis was?!

   And which exhortation does Paul repeat (verse 4)?

2. At this point in chapter 4 of Philippians, Paul begins a series of rapid-fire exhortations. Note the four in this passage:

Verse 4: "Rejoice in the Lord always..." What difference does rejoicing in the Lord—and always!—make when it comes to personal peace?

Verse 5: "Let your gentleness be known to all men..." Gentleness has also been translated "moderation," "forbearance," "reasonableness," and "graciousness." It is exemplified in one who is "ready to forgive" and possesses a "fairmindedness." Thus, it calls us as Christians to be characterized as gentle and forbearing in our attitudes toward others. We should exhibit a spirit of willingness to yield under trial—a refusal to retaliate when attacked.[18] How in the world can we do that? Answer: "The Lord is at hand." He will judge on our behalf and make right any wrong-suffering we endure at the hands of others.

Verse 6: "Be anxious for nothing..." These words must have induced such hope, encouragement, and peace in the lives of the Philippian believers! "Be anxious for nothing"! When we are anxious, we're not trusting God will care for us. In fact, anxiety or lack of trust is a species of "unconscious blasphemy" against Him. How high is your anxiety level, and how high is your "trust" level?

Verse 6: "...but...let your requests be made known to God..." Instead of being anxious and failing to trust God, we are to let our requests be known to Him, to exercise our faith. We are to pray to the Lord and lay out our "needs" and our precise petitions before Him.

3. And what will be the result of the above process (verse 7)?

...and into your heart

How are you doing in the areas of Paul's four commands? Check it out.

✓ Are you joyful? When do you most need to "rejoice in the Lord"?

✓ Are you gracious? Think of a person who challenges you most in this all-important area of forbearance. How are you encouraged by knowing that "the Lord is at hand"?

✓ Do you suffer from anxiety? Or, is there a particular instance in your day-in, day-out life that tends to breed anxiety in you?

✓ How do you think praying will and can and does help such a situation? Is there anything that keeps you from praying?

And finally, are you enjoying the peaceful spirit Paul says is possible for you and me? If not, determine to follow Paul's steps toward experiencing God's peace: Be joyful, be gracious, be anxious for nothing, be praying, and then the peace of God, which surpasses all understanding, will guard your heart and mind through Christ Jesus!

Heart Response

Dear one, when we think of all we want in life, I know joy is one thing we both yearn for. So is peace. And here in our Bible, in the God-breathed, inspired Word of God which comes straight from the mind and heart of God, we have the source of both! But to enjoy these two desired qualities of life, we must follow Paul's "to-do" list:

Rejoice. This is not an option, my friend. This is a command! It's an exhortation to cheerfulness. The Greek language translates, "Keep on rejoicing in the Lord always...no matter what." And it's true: We are to rejoice *in the Lord*, no matter what is happening to us. As D. L. Moody wrote in the 1800s,

> *C*hristians, it is your duty not only to be good, but to shine.... Even in your deepest griefs, rejoice in God. As waves' phosphoresce, let joys flash from the swing of the sorrows of your souls."[19]
>
> —D. L. Moody

Pray. This, too, is not an option, but is also commanded of us! Rather than suffering from anxious care, we should present our needs to the Lord. In any and all circumstances, we are to lay our requests before God.

And the results? The sweet, sweet results? First, not only will God respond to our prayers, but the immediate result will be that we will experience "the peace of God"—that is, a peace that is characteristic of God Himself. Even when our circumstances do not change, God's peace prevails. And second, God's peace will stand guard like a soldier or a sentinel against all the anxieties that normally attack our heart and mind.

So pray, dear one! Prayer is requisite in every providence and perfumes every relation. It is through prayer that we truly experience God's peace which surpasses all comprehension!

Lesson 21

Thinking on God's Truths

Philippians 4:8-9

I's a fact that the conscious human mind is always thinking about something! And, if a man thinks of something often enough, he'll end up not being able to stop thinking about it.[20] Are you familiar with the admonition, "Sow a thought, reap an action; sow an action, reap a habit; sow a habit, reap a character; sow a character, reap a destiny"? And how did this destiny come to be? It all began with a thought!

Our thought life is vital to finding peace, dear one. Paul knew that. He exhorts us in this lesson to guide and guard our thoughts. Then his goal—peace for each member in a church and peace in the church—would be realized. He wanted all believers to know and enjoy "the peace of God" (4:7) and "the God of peace" (verse 9).

Read on now, and taste the ingredients that should make up the content of our thoughts. And then, as Paul states, "meditate [or think] on these things."

Philippians 4:8-9

8 Finally, brethren, whatever things are true, whatever things are noble, whatever things are just, whatever things are pure, whatever things are lovely, whatever things are of good report, if there is any virtue and if there is anything praiseworthy—meditate on these things.

9 The things which you learned and received and heard and saw in me, these do, and the God of peace will be with you.

Out of God's Word...

1. Paul is pressing toward a goal of finishing his epistle to his dear friends in Philippi, and comes to the word finally. He's been pushing his readers (and you and me, too!) to achieve inner peace so that they could enjoy peace amongst themselves in the church. Paul knew that if inner tranquility is to be continually enjoyed and its influence shed abroad, certain steps must be taken. So he tells his readers what to think, what to take into account, what to meditate and reflect upon, so that the things thought upon could then shape their conduct.[21] What are the eight conditions Paul sets for biblical thinking (verse 8)?

   a.   e.

   b.   f.

   c.   g.

   d.   h.

2. Paul exhorts his friends not only about their thought life and what they should be careful to think upon, but also about the examples they should be careful to emulate and follow. List the four criteria he sets in verse 9 that will help the Philippians discern who to follow.

a.

b.

c.

d.

What admonition does he then give (verse 9)?

And what will be the result of following his advice (verse 9)?

...and into your heart

- As one gentleman writes, "Every thought of heavenly things contributes to the making of character. Those who enthrone Christ in the sanctuary of the mind will stop gravitating and will reach out for the characteristics seen in His life."[22] Can you think of an everyday-life example for several of the characteristics Paul notes where thinking on "these things" would advance you in your quest to be like Jesus?

True (as opposed to false, also the gospel-truth)

Noble (dignified, honorable, and worthy of honor)

Just (what is due)

Pure (morally undefiled)

Lovely (pleasing and attractive, winsome)

Of good report (speaking well of, something fit for God to hear)

Virtuous (excellent)

Praiseworthy (anything that calls down God's approval, anything worthy of praise)

- Looking at these virtues and their meanings again, can you pinpoint an area for change in your own thought life?

- Can you think of what you could meditate and think upon that would most definitely measure up to *all* of Paul's criteria?

- Could you say Paul's words from verse 9—"The things which you learned and received and heard and saw in me, these do"—to your children (or grandchildren)? Your friends? Your neighbors? Your co-workers?

- What steps could you take toward becoming the credible person Paul speaks of in verse 9?

Heart Response

Whatsoever things that are true, noble, just, pure, lovely, befitting, virtuous, and praiseworthy—think on these things. Wow! Paul is giving us a tall order here! Are you wondering *how* we can possibly follow through on this counsel? As I prayed through these eight aspects of Christian thought life, I came up with three of "these things" you and I can think about, knowing that they meet these criteria.

First, we can think about God. When we meditate on the person of God and His attributes, we are thinking on these things. When we ponder the depth of the riches of the wisdom and knowledge of God and His goodness and grace to us, we are thinking on these things. When we consider the protection and provision God lavishly grants to us as His children, we are thinking on these things. When we think about the many promises of God extended to us, we are thinking on these things.

Second, we can think about Jesus Christ. Oh, the sweet, sweet Savior! When we recall the prophecies and plan of God pointing to Jesus' appearance, we are thinking on these things. When we reflect on the Gospel accounts of the life of Christ—from His nativity to His death and resurrection and ascension—we are thinking on these things. When we contemplate what Jesus' life and death accomplished for us and our position in Him as New Testament believers, we are thinking on these things.

Third, we can think about the Word of God. As the psalmist declared, the law of the Lord is perfect, sure, right, pure, clean, true, righteous...and sweeter than honey and the honeycomb (Psalm 19:7-11). Yes, when we are thinking on God's Word, we are thinking on these things.

Beloved, when we have three such lofty "things" as God, His Son, and His Word to think about, why would we want to think on anything else? O worship now...and think on these things!

Lesson 22

Coping with Life's Circumstances

Philippians 4:10-14

*P*aul lived in the day of the Stoics, a group that based their ethics and morals upon pride, independence, and fate. The Stoic, therefore, was one who considered himself to be "self-sufficient." But Paul, the humble servant and prisoner of the Lord, considered himself to be "God-sufficient." His confidence was always and securely rooted in the Lord and His sovereign providence over his life. Paul could face anything, not because he was like the Stoic and not because he was competent, but because, in every situation, he had Christ. As a man who walked with Christ, Paul could cope with anything!

Today's lesson brings us hope and encouragement in all that we are presently facing and instructions in trust and contentment for anything the future may hold for us. Heed Paul's powerful words...and learn along with him the secret to contentment!

Philippians 4:10-14

¹⁰ But I rejoiced in the Lord greatly that now at last your care for me has flourished again; though you surely did care, but you lacked opportunity.

¹¹ Not that I speak in regard to need, for I have learned in whatever state I am, to be content:

¹² I know how to be abased, and I know how to abound. Everywhere and in all things I have learned both to be full and to be hungry, both to abound and to suffer need.

¹³ I can do all things through Christ who strengthens me.

¹⁴ Nevertheless you have done well that you shared in my distress.

Out of God's Word...

1. After instructing the Philippians to "rejoice in the Lord" (4:4), Paul himself now rejoices. What caused him to rejoice (verse 10)?

2. What important lesson had Paul learned in the meantime (verse 11)?

3. To define for his Philippian readers exactly what he had learned, Paul used couplets of opposites (verse 12). List them here.

a.

b.

c.

4. And exactly what does Paul say is his secret for living in these and in all circumstances (verse 13)?

...*and into your heart*

- This study of Philippians has been about experiencing God's peace, and we've seen how our thoughts lead us to peace of mind and to the peace of God, regardless of our situation or circumstances. When our heart is transformed into a sanctuary of spiritual loveliness because of thinking on the spiritually lovely things Paul notes in 4:8, then that condition extends itself to encompass our life conditions and we experience the peace of contentment. What do you learn about contentment from Paul's words?

- Is there an area of discontent or lack of peace in your life where you can apply Paul's principles of contentment to work and receive God's promised strength?

- Is it possible that you could be the resource God uses in meeting the needs of another? Pray about showing your care and concern for the distresses of others.

Heart Response

Consider where Paul was while writing these eternal words of encouragement. He's being held under house arrest (Acts 20:30). He's in the midst of a life-and-death trial. And yet his acceptance of God's will for his life exudes from his place of bondage. Yes, as he testifies, Paul had learned in whatever state he was in—and that included being under arrest!—to be content.

Just as he had always found Christ's strength sufficient for all he endured and for all of his tasks, Paul continues to find the strength that a vital union with Christ supplies to be adequate for maintaining his apostolic work and persevering in spite of each day's suffering.

Dear one, not one day goes by that I do not at some point of looming discouragement or despair remember and recite and remind myself of Philippians 4:13. It's amazing that as we as God's children look to His Word and His promises and His strength, He graciously—every time and without fail!—provides the strength we need to take just one more step along our God-ordained path. In fact, we must learn to simply fill in the blank: "I can do all things—including this [whatever "this" is]—through Christ who strengthens me." So, as we leave this good-for-what-ails-you passage, let's take a few instructions along with us: Be sure to...

Learn as Paul did that you, too, can do, endure, complete, cope with, and manage all things through Christ who also strengthens you. As one who enjoys a personal union with the Lord, you can face life—each and every day of it as well as all of it—victoriously. How? Because Christ is in you and extends His grace and strength to you. Learn it, beloved! Count on it. And put it to use at every opportunity.

Look to the Lord for His strength. He is the mapmaker who designed the path of your life. He knows the beginning and the end of it. You can trust God to bring you to His expected end, through the good plan He has for your life (Jeremiah 29:11).

Live out—in front of your family and friends—your confidence in God and your contentment in every situation. Paul had just instructed the Philippians to look at him as he lived out his faith. Your family, too, needs a shining example of what it means to know and to trust the Lord.

Love others by giving and sharing what you have. This is one of the wonderful lessons for us here in this passage. Even though Paul was content, still God used the Philippian believers to meet his needs. So, go...and do likewise!

Giving God's Way

Philippians 4:15-19

George Müller was a British man who opened and operated an orphanage in the mid-1800s on a faith basis. For 40 years, George Müller literally prayed food into the mouths of his up-to-2,000 orphans each day. He fervently prayed to God, the One who had promised to supply all his needs. In the end, Müller's 2,000 orphans were cared for, given a happy home, and instructed in the Christian life. Yes, this dear saint lived his life on the receiving end of others' giving. Some days he refused to get up off his office floor where he knelt praying until a worker would gently tap on his door to let him know that God had once again supplied, that food had arrived from yet another source...for one more day. When George Müller died, though he had handled over eight million dollars sent in for the orphan work, he possessed only a meager amount of personal goods.

Giving and receiving. You and I, dear one, are asked to do the former and promised the latter. O, what a wonderful God we have who logs positively into our spiritual account as we give, and generously provides for any and all our needs after we've given! This is giving—and receiving—God's way!

See it yourself in Paul's wonderful words.

Philippians 4:15-19

¹⁵ Now you Philippians know also that in the beginning of the gospel, when I departed from Macedonia, no church shared with me concerning giving and receiving but you only.

¹⁶ For even in Thessalonica you sent aid once and again for my necessities.

¹⁷ Not that I seek the gift, but I seek the fruit that abounds to your account.

¹⁸ Indeed I have all and abound. I am full, having received from Epaphroditus the things which were sent from you, a sweet-smelling aroma, an acceptable sacrifice, well pleasing to God.

¹⁹ And my God shall supply all your need according to His riches in glory by Christ Jesus.

Out of God's Word...

1. As you ponder this lesson's scriptures, note what the Philippians had done that no other church had done (verse 15).

How often had they done it (verse 16)?

And what was the purpose of their "gift" (verse 16)?

2. It's always nice to receive gifts and aid and assistance, but what was Paul's primary desire for the Philippians (verse 17)?

3. From Paul's perspective, what had the giving hearts of the Philippians accomplished (verse 18)?

And from God's perspective (verse 18)?

4. Sometimes we withhold our goods and assets because we are afraid that if we give them away to others, we ourselves will lack! But Paul put this fear to rest. What does he tell the Philippians about God that should dispel all worry (verse 19)?

...*and into your heart*

• In a very real sense, every gift is an act of faith. Since our natural inclination is to hoard, save, invest, and look out for and take care of ourselves, loosening our fingers from their clutch on our worldly goods is truly an act of faith. Why? Because when we give our resources away, we must trust in the Lord to take care of us. How would you rate your trust in Him and His gracious, adequate, glorious, promised provision, dear friend? Do you give freely (Matthew 10:8), seeking to help those in need? Do you give joyfully (2 Corinthians 9:7)? Have you yet experienced the fact that it is more blessed to give than to receive (Acts 20:35)? Take a few minutes before the Lord and write down some honest answers.

* And now for God's promise in verse 19: Do you believe that your God will supply all that you truly need? Jot down a few more honest answers.

* It's good to look into the mirror of our soul, isn't it? To see what we really do think and believe and why? We've just seen Paul relate to giving as a spiritual issue, as an act that bears spiritual fruit in our lives and pleases God. Our giving, Paul says, issues forth a sweet-smelling aroma and is an acceptable sacrifice to our Lord. Can you note a few of your plans in this vital matter of giving to meet the needs of others?

Heart Response

As we log this life-changing, faith-inducing lesson on giving God's way, I'm thinking about two wonderful people who lived by God's giving-and-receiving formula.

First there was the husband, C. T. Studd, whom we met in Lesson 14. C. T. Studd, like Paul, left the privileged life he had enjoyed before becoming a Christian. Extremely wealthy and Cambridge-educated, Studd was one of the seven men from that college who began the world missions movement in the nineteenth century. As these men left for China, a news correspondent described them as "standing side by side renouncing the careers in which they had already gained no small distinction, putting aside the splendid prizes of earthly ambition, taking leave of the social circles in which they shone with no mean brilliance, and plunging into that warfare whose splendours are seen only by faith, and whose rewards seem so shadowy to the unopened vision of ordinary men."[23]

Then there was the wife. Just before leaving on his second trip to China, C. T. Studd "invested in the Bank of heaven by giving away all of his inheritance" except for 3,400 British pounds which he presented to his bride before their wedding. She, too, knew about forgetting what lies behind. She asked, "Now, Charlie, what did the Lord tell the rich young man to do?" When C. T. answered, "Sell all," she said, "Well, then, we will start clear with the Lord at our wedding." She then anonymously gave the 3,400 pounds to General Booth of the Salvation Army.[24] Both C. T. Studd and his bride knew that their God would supply all their need according to His riches in glory by Christ Jesus! And, indeed, from 1883 until Mr. Studd's death in 1931—for nearly 50 years—God did exactly that!

Would that you and I would be so giving and that fruit would abound to our accounts in heaven! May we ever offer our goods and means to those in need. And may our heavenly Father ever enjoy the sweet-smelling aroma of our sacrifice!

Lesson 24

Beginnings and Endings

As a writer I've been learning the skill of bringing each chapter of a book to a conclusion and the book itself together at its end. To wrap it up, so to speak. To tie up all the loose ends. To finish weaving together all of the various strands that make up my message.

Well, here in this final passage of Philippians, we see Paul (indeed, he's a master writer!) doing just that. He reaches back to the opening statements of this letter to tie up his thoughts here at the end of this book with common threads. And when he's done, we have a beautiful, complete, gift-wrapped (and with a tied ribbon bow!) package from Paul to enjoy over and over and over again.

Read these final four verses from the pen of Paul and allow them to lift your soul and spirit upward. They are indeed full of grace and glory!

Philippians 4:20-23

²⁰ Now to our God and Father be glory forever and ever. Amen.

²¹ Greet every saint in Christ Jesus. The brethren who are with me greet you.

²² All the saints greet you, but especially those who are of Caesar's household.

²³ The grace of our Lord Jesus Christ be with you all. Amen.

Out of God's Word...

1. Having written about God in Philippians 4:19 (see the previous lesson), Paul now breaks forth into an exclamation of pure praise. What possessive pronoun does Paul use regarding God in verse 20?

2. One thread Paul gathers up here at the end of his epistle is a mention of those who are with him (verse 21). Who were some of those brethren, according to Philippians 1:1 and 2:25?

3. Another of Paul's common threads for beginning and ending his letter is the concept of "saint" and "saints." Note the special category of saints mentioned in verse 22. Who are they?

Do you remember Lesson 5 and how Paul pointed out to his friends and readers that the awful things that had happened to him had turned out for good, for the furtherance of the gospel? He mentioned then that the whole of Caesar's palace guard knew of his faith in Jesus Christ. And now what appears to have happened in Caesar's own household (verse 22)?

(As one scholarly gentleman has so eloquently noted, "The crucified Galilean carpenter had already begun to rule those who ruled the greatest empire in the world."[25])

4. Ah, and then there is the great grace of our great God! The Christian life, which is an expression of grace, is by grace sustained. The final verse to some extent summarizes all of Paul's yearnings for those Christians at Philippi who had manifested their love and care for him. How does Paul begin his letter (Philippians 1:2)? And how does he end it (Philippians 4:23)?

...and into your heart

- Above all else, the apostle Paul wants his friends in the Philippian church to experience God's peace—peace among themselves, peace of heart, peace of mind, and peace in relation to earthly things and circumstances. How does each verse in Paul's blessing or benediction bring you peace?

Verse 20—Now to our God and Father be glory forever and ever. Amen.

Verse 21—Greet every saint in Christ Jesus. The brethren who are with me greet you.

Verse 22—All the saints greet you, but especially those who are of Caesar's household.

Verse 23—The grace of our Lord Jesus Christ be with you all. Amen.

As still another Christian thinker adds regarding Paul's benediction and our peace, "If this pronouncement is accepted with a believing heart, then from this basic blessing of grace all others flow forth, filling the very spirit...with the peace of God that surpasses all understanding!"[26]

Heart Response

As our hearts and souls ring with Paul's blessing, it's good to remember three things:

First, Paul's words do indeed bless us, which reminds us of the power of our own words spoken or written to bring grace to those we address. Our tongue—and our pen—possess the power to encourage, calm, fortify, and soothe the souls of others. You and I have both experienced the wounds inflicted by harsh words or venomous letters. Let's make sure we, like Paul, are God's messengers of grace!

Second, Paul reached those around him with the good news of Jesus Christ. His constant companions were soldiers in Caesar's guard, the Praetorian Guard, the Imperial Guard of Rome. Yes, Paul was chained to them...but they in turn were chained to Paul! And Paul took advantage of such opportunities to share about Jesus Christ until he could write that some in Caesar's household had become saints. Are you aware of your opportunities, dear one? You, too, can tell others about Jesus—even the most unlikely ones!

And *third*, dear Paul never lost sight of the fact that our entire salvation—from start to finish—depends on God's sovereign favor in Jesus Christ. He is worthy of our praise; He is worthy of our exaltation; He is worthy to be talked about; He is worthy of our worship; and He is worthy of glory forever and ever!

And now, may the grace of our Lord Jesus Christ be with *you!* Amen.

*L*esson 25

Looking Back...
and Moving Forward

Philippians Review

*C*ongratulations, dear friend. You have just finished exploring the entire book of Philippians. So small, yet so packed with life-changing truths!

The book of Philippians has several veins of gold running through it. Take a few minutes to think through each chapter, and then write your main thoughts based on what you have learned about:

Chapter 1: Thinking about life and death

Summary: In chapter one, Paul, the optimistic prisoner, "expresses his deep conviction that whatever happens to him, whether it be life or death, acquittal or condemnation, Christ will be magnified in his person. Though he desires to be with Christ, regarding this as being very far better, yet he is willing to place the need of the Philippians above his own immediate enjoyment of eternal bliss."[27]

Chapter 2: Looking to the example of Christ's humility

Summary: In chapter two, Paul, the pastor, first calls his congregation in Philippi to oneness, lowliness, and helpfulness, and then points to our dear Savior as the ultimate example of true humility. In Christ this lovely spirit of lowliness and humility has been beautifully exemplified. Paul's reasoning went like this: "If Christ Jesus humbled himself so deeply, the Philippians [and we, too] should surely be willing to humble themselves in their own small way. If he became obedient to the extent of death by a cross, then they [and we] in their own small way should be obedient to His directives. And, if He was rewarded, then so will they [and we] be rewarded."[28]

Chapter 3: Losing all to gain the knowledge of Christ

Summary: "I counted...and I count" (verses 7-8). Do you remember the day, dear one, when the light of the Lord broke in upon you? In the words of the great preacher G. Campbell Morgan, "It was a very real thing. It changed all our outlook. It compelled us to reconsideration of all the facts of life. We obeyed. We turned our backs upon all sorts of gains, counting them as merely worthless things. We yielded to the call and glory of the life in Christ. It was all excellent."[29] We must be sure we are continuing to count all things loss for the excellence of Christ Jesus our Lord!

Chapter 4: Being content in Christ

Summary: When Paul wrote that he had learned, in whatever state he was, to be content, he meant something of this sort: "The satisfaction of a material need must not be construed as being either the real reason for or the measure of my joy. On the contrary, regardless of outward circumstances, I would still be satisfied. My conversion-experience, and also my subsequent trials for the sake of Christ and His gospel, have taught me a lesson. The path which I traveled led me ever closer to Christ, to His love, and to His power, yes to Christ and contentment in Him. That very contentment is riches to me."[30] Could you say the same, dear sister?

Heart Response

And now it's time for the most important "Heart Response" you'll make in this book. It's time to make sure that you truly belong to Christ, that you are truly in the family of God, that you're a Christian who enjoys the peace of God and the God of Peace.

So I must ask you: Are you a child of God? Have you been reconciled to God through His Son, Jesus Christ?

Just to be sure the path to God is clear, prayerfully consider these facts:

1. The fact of sin—Romans 3:23 states, "All have sinned and fall short of the glory of God."

2. The fact of judgment—Romans 6:23 teaches us that "the wages of sin is death, but the gift of God is eternal life in Christ Jesus our Lord."

3. The fact of Christ's death for sins— Romans 5:8 tells us that "God demonstrates His own love towards us, in that while we were yet sinners, Christ died for us."

4. The fact of acceptance of Christ by faith—Romans 10:9 shows us the way: "If you confess with your mouth Jesus as Lord, and believe in your heart that God raised Him from the dead, you shall be saved."

5. The fact of peace—Romans 5:8 tells us that "having been justified by faith, we have peace with God through our Lord Jesus Christ."

If you're not yet God's child, ask God to open your heart to these truths so that you may experience and enjoy God's perfect peace.

And if you're already a child of God, make your "heart response" one of thanksgiving and praise to God for the peace He extends to you through His Son, Jesus Christ.

As we end this sweet epistle of peace, dear one, may you experience Christ as your portion and happiness! May you know firsthand what it means to live in Christ, to let the mind of Christ be in you, to know Christ, and to rest in the peace of His provision of your every need, now...and forever. Amen.

How to Study the Bible —Some Practical Tips

By Jim George, Th.M.

One of the noblest pursuits a child of God can embark upon is to get to know and understand God better. The best way we can accomplish this is to look carefully at the book He has written, the Bible, which communicates who He is and His plan for mankind. There are a number of ways we can study the Bible, but one of the most effective and simple approaches to reading and understanding God's Word involves three simple steps:

Step 1: Observation—*What does the passage say?*

Step 2: Interpretation—*What does the passage mean?*

Step 3: Application—*What am I going to do about what the passage says and means?*

Observation is the first and most important step in the process. As you read the Bible text, you need to *look* carefully at what is said, and how. Look for:

- *Terms, not words.* Words can have many meanings, but terms are words used in a specific way in a specific context. (For instance, the word *trunk* could apply to a tree, a car, or a storage box. However, when you read, "That tree has a very large trunk," you know exactly what the word means, which makes it a term.)

- *Structure.* If you look at your Bible, you will see that the text has units called *paragraphs* (indented or marked ¶). A paragraph is a complete unit of thought. You can discover the content of the author's message by noting and understanding each paragraph unit.

- *Emphasis*. The amount of space or the number of chapters or verses devoted to a specific topic will reveal the importance of that topic (for example, note the emphasis of Romans 9–11 and Psalm 119).

- *Repetition*. This is another way an author demonstrates that something is important. One reading of 1 Corinthians 13, where the author uses the word "love" nine times in only 13 verses, communicates to us that love is the focal point of these 13 verses.

- *Relationships between ideas*. Pay close attention, for example, to certain relationships that appear in the text:

  —Cause-and-effect: "Well done, good and faithful servant; you were faithful over a few things, I will make you ruler over many things" (Matthew 25:21).
  —Ifs and thens: "If My people who are called by My name will humble themselves, and pray and seek My face, and turn from their wicked ways, then I will hear from heaven and forgive their sin and heal their land" (2 Chronicles 7:14).
  —Questions and answers: "Who is the King of glory? The Lord strong and mighty" (Psalm 24:8).

- *Comparisons and contrasts*. For example, "You have heard that it was said...but I say to you..." (Matthew 5:21).

- *Literary form*. The Bible is literature, and the three main types of literature in the Bible are discourse (the epistles), prose (Old Testament history), and poetry (the Psalms). Considering the type of literature makes a great deal of difference when you read and interpret the Scriptures.

- *Atmosphere*. The author had a particular reason or burden for writing each passage, chapter, and book. Be sure you notice the mood or tone or urgency of the writing.

After you have considered these things, you then are ready to ask the "Wh" questions:

Who?	Who are the people in this passage?
What?	What is happening in this passage?
Where?	Where is this story taking place?
When?	What time (of day, of the year, in history) is it?

Asking these four "Wh" questions can help you notice terms and identify atmosphere. The answers will also enable you to use your imagination to recreate the scene you're reading about.

As you answer the "Wh" questions and imagine the event, you'll probably come up with some questions of your own. Asking those additional questions for understanding will help to build a bridge between observation (the first step) and interpretation (the second step) of the Bible study process.

Interpretation is discovering the meaning of a passage, the author's main thought or idea. Answering the questions that arise during observation will help you in the process of interpretation. Five clues (called "the five C's") can help you determine the author's main point(s):

Context. You can answer 75 percent of your questions about a passage when you read the text. Reading the text involves looking at the near context (the verse immediately before and after) as well as the far context (the paragraph or the chapter that precedes and/or follows the passage you're studying).

Cross-references. Let Scripture interpret Scripture. That is, let other passages in the Bible shed light on the passage you are looking at. At the same time, be careful not to assume that the same word or phrase in two different passages means the same thing.

Culture. The Bible was written long ago, so when we interpret it, we need to understand it from the writers' cultural context.

Conclusion. Having answered your questions for understanding by means of context, cross-reference, and culture, you can make a preliminary statement of the passage's meaning. Remember that if your passage consists of more than one paragraph, the author may be presenting more than one thought or idea.

Consultation. Reading books known as commentaries, which are written by Bible scholars, can help you interpret Scripture.

Application is why we study the Bible. We want our lives to change; we want to be obedient to God and to grow more like Jesus Christ. After we have observed a passage and interpreted or understood it to the best of our ability, we must then apply its truth to our own life.

You'll want to ask the following questions of every passage of Scripture you study:

- How does the truth revealed here affect my relationship with God?
- How does this truth affect my relationship with others?
- How does this truth affect me?
- How does this truth affect my response to the enemy Satan?

The application step is not completed by simply answering these questions; the key is *putting into practice* what God has taught you in your study. Although at any given moment you cannot be consciously applying *every*thing you're learning in Bible study, you can be consciously applying *some*thing. And when you work on applying a truth to your life, God will bless your efforts by, as noted earlier, conforming you to the image of Jesus Christ.

Helpful Bible Study Resources:

Concordance—Young's or Strong's

Bible dictionary—Unger's or Holman's

Webster's dictionary

The Zondervan Pictorial Encyclopedia of the Bible

Manners and Customs of the Bible,
  James M. Freeman

Books on Bible Study:

The Joy of Discovery, Oletta Wald

Enjoy Your Bible, Irving L. Jensen

How to Read the Bible for All It's Worth, Gordon
Fee & Douglas Stuart

A Layman's Guide to Interpreting the Bible,
  W. Henrichsen

$\mathscr{L}$eading a Bible Study Discussion Group

$\mathscr{W}$hat a privilege it is to lead a Bible study! And what joy and excitement await you as you delve into the Word of God and help others to discover its life-changing truths. If God has called you to lead a Bible study group, I know you'll be spending much time in prayer and planning and giving much thought to being an effective leader. I also know that taking the time to read through the following tips will help you to navigate the challenges of leading a Bible study discussion group and enjoying the effort and opportunity.

The Leader's Roles

As a Bible study group leader, you'll find your role changing back and forth from *expert* to *cheerleader* to *lover* to *referee* during the course of a session.

Since you're the leader, group members will look to you to be the *expert* guiding them through the material. So be well prepared. In fact, be over-prepared so that you know the material better than any group member does. Start your study early in the week and let its message simmer all week long. (You might even work several lessons ahead so that you have in mind the big picture and the overall direction of the study.) Be ready to share some additional gems that your group members wouldn't have discovered on their own. That extra insight from your study time—or that comment from a wise Bible teacher or scholar, that clever saying, that keen observation from another believer, and even an appropriate joke—adds an element of fun and keeps Bible study from becoming routine, monotonous, and dry.

Second, be ready to be the group's *cheerleader*. Your energy and enthusiasm for the task at hand can be contagious. It can also stimulate people to get more involved in their personal study as well as in the group discussion.

Third, be the *lover,* the one who shows a genuine concern for the members of the group. You're the one who will establish the atmosphere of the group. If you laugh and have fun, the group members will laugh and have fun. If you hug, they will hug. If you care, they will care. If you share, they will share. If you love, they will love. So pray every day to love the women God has placed in your group. Ask Him to show you how to love them with His love.

Finally, as the leader, you'll need to be the *referee* on occasion. That means making sure everyone has an equal opportunity to speak. That's easier to do when you operate under the assumption that every member of the group has something worthwhile to contribute. So, trusting that the Lord has taught each person during the week, act on that assumption.

Expert, cheerleader, lover, and referee—these four roles of the leader may make the task seem overwhelming. But that's not bad if it keeps you on your knees praying for your group.

A Good Start

Beginning on time, greeting people warmly, and opening in prayer gets the study off to a good start. Know what you want to have happen during your time together and make sure those things get done. That kind of order means comfort for those involved.

Establish a format and let the group members know what that format is. People appreciate being in a Bible study that focuses on the Bible. So keep the discussion on the topic and move the group through the questions. Tangents are often hard to avoid—and even harder to rein in. So be sure to focus on the answers to questions about the specific passage at hand. After all, the purpose of the group is Bible study!

Finally, as someone has accurately observed, "Personal growth is one of the by-products of any effective small group. This growth is achieved when people are recognized and accepted by others. The more friendliness, mutual trust, respect, and warmth exhibited, the more likely that the member will find pleasure in the group, and, too, the more likely she will work hard toward the accomplishment of the group's goals. The effective leader will strive to reinforce desirable traits" (source unknown).

A Dozen Helpful Tips

Here is a list of helpful suggestions for leading a Bible study discussion group:

1. Arrive early, ready to focus fully on others and give of yourself. If you have to do any last-minute preparation, review, re-grouping, or praying, do it in the car. Don't dash in, breathless, harried, late, still tweaking your plans.

2. Check out your meeting place in advance. Do you have everything you need—tables, enough chairs, a blackboard, hymnals if you plan to sing, coffee, etc.?

3. Greet each person warmly by name as she arrives. After all, you've been praying for these women all week long, so let each VIP know that you're glad she's arrived.

4. Use name tags for at least the first two or three weeks.

5. Start on time no matter what—even if only one person is there!

6. Develop a pleasant but firm opening statement. You might say, "This lesson was great! Let's get started so we can enjoy all of it!" or "Let's pray before we begin our lesson."

7. Read the questions, but don't hesitate to reword them on occasion. Rather than reading an entire paragraph of instructions, for instance, you might say, "Question 1 asks us to list some ways that Christ displayed humility. Lisa, please share one way Christ displayed humility."

8. Summarize or paraphrase the answers given. Doing so will keep the discussion focused on the topic; eliminate digressions; help avoid or clear up any misunderstandings of the text; and keep each group member aware of what the others are saying.

9. Keep moving and don't add any of your own questions to the discussion time. It's important to get through the study guide questions. So if a cut-and-dried answer is called for, you don't need to comment with anything other than a "thank you." But when the question asks for an opinion or an application (for instance, "How can this truth help us in our marriages?" or "How do *you* find time for your quiet time?"), let all who want to contribute.

10. Affirm each person who contributes, especially if the contribution was very personal, painful to share, or a quiet person's rare statement. Make everyone who shares a hero by saying something like "Thank you for sharing that insight from your own life" or "We certainly appreciate what God has taught you. Thank you for letting us in on it."

11. Watch your watch, put a clock right in front of you, or consider using a timer. Pace the discussion so that you meet your cut-off time, especially if you want time to pray. Stop at the designated time even if you haven't finished the lesson. Remember that everyone has worked through the study once; you are simply going over it again.

12. End on time. You can only make friends with your group members by ending on time or even a little early! Besides,

members of your group have the next item on their agenda to attend to—picking up children from the nursery, babysitter, or school; heading home to tend to matters there; running errands; getting to bed; or spending some time with their husbands. So let them out *on time!*

Five Common Problems

In any group, you can anticipate certain problems. Here are some common ones that can arise, along with helpful solutions:

1. *The incomplete lesson*—Right from the start, establish the policy that if someone has not done the lesson, it is best for her not to answer the questions. But do try to include her responses to questions that ask for opinions or experiences. Everyone can share some thoughts in reply to a question like, "Reflect on what you know about both athletic and spiritual training and then share what you consider to be the essential elements of training oneself in godliness."

2. *The gossip*—The Bible clearly states that gossiping is wrong, so you don't want to allow it in your group. Set a high and strict standard by saying, "I am not comfortable with this conversation," or "We [not *you*] are gossiping, ladies. Let's move on."

3. *The talkative member*—Here are three scenarios and some possible solutions for each.

   a. The problem talker may be talking because she has done her homework and is excited about something she has to share. She may also know more about the subject than the others and, if you cut her off, the rest of the group may suffer.

   SOLUTION: Respond with a comment like: "Sarah, you are making very valuable contributions. Let's see if we

can get some reactions from the others," or "I know Sarah can answer this. She's really done her homework. How about some of the rest of you?"

b. The talkative member may be talking because she has *not* done her homework and wants to contribute, but she has no boundaries.
SOLUTION: Establish at the first meeting that those who have not done the lesson do not contribute except on opinion or application questions. You may need to repeat this guideline at the beginning of each session.

c. The talkative member may want to be heard whether or not she has anything worthwhile to contribute.
SOLUTION: After subtle reminders, be more direct, saying, "Betty, I know you would like to share your ideas, but let's give others a chance. I'll call on you later."

4. *The quiet member*—Here are two scenarios and possible solutions.

a. The quiet member wants the floor but somehow can't get the chance to share.
SOLUTION: Clear the path for the quiet member by first watching for clues that she wants to speak (moving to the edge of her seat, looking as if she wants to speak, perhaps even starting to say something) and then saying, "Just a second. I think Chris wants to say something." Then, of course, make her a hero!

b. The quiet member simply doesn't want the floor.
SOLUTION: "Chris, what answer do you have on question 2?" or "Chris, what do you think about...?" Usually after a shy person has contributed a few times, she will become more confident and more ready to share. Your role is to provide an opportunity where there is *no* risk of a wrong answer. But occasionally a group member will tell you that she would rather not be called on. Honor her

request, but from time to time ask her privately if she feels ready to contribute to the group discussions.

In fact, give all your group members the right to pass. During your first meeting, explain that any time a group member does not care to share an answer, she may simply say, "I pass." You'll want to repeat this policy at the beginning of every group session.

5. *The wrong answer*—Never tell a group member that she has given a wrong answer, but at the same time never let a wrong answer go by.

SOLUTION: Either ask if someone else has a different answer or ask additional questions that will cause the right answer to emerge. As the women get closer to the right answer, say, "We're getting warmer! Keep thinking! We're almost there!"

Learning from Experience

Immediately after each Bible study session, evaluate the group discussion time using this checklist. You may also want a member of your group (or an assistant or trainee or outside observer) to evaluate you periodically.

Notes

1. Taken from *A Woman After God's Own Heart*® (Eugene, OR: Harvest House Publishers), pp. 24-29.

2. *Life Applications from Every Chapter of the Bible* (Grand Rapids MI: Fleming H. Revell, 1926, 1994), p. 330.

3. *365 Life Lessons from Bible People* (Wheaton IL: Tyndale House Publishers, Inc., 1996), p. 325.

4. Paul Rees, as cited in Albert M. Wells, Jr., *Inspiring Quotations Contemporary and Classical* (Nashville, TN: Thomas Nelson, 1988) p. 160.

5. John F. Walvoord, *Philippians—Triumph in Christ* (Chicago: Moody Press, 1977), p. 40.

6. William Hendriksen, *New Testament Commentary—Exposition of Philippians* (Grand Rapids, MI: Baker Book House, 1975), p. 78.

7. Jim Elliot *Inspiring Quotations—Contemporary & Classical* (Nashville: Thomas Nelson Publishers,1988), p. 178.

8. Matthew Henry, *Matthew Henry's Commentary on the Whole Bible*—Vol. 6 (Peabody, MA: Hendrickson Publishers, 1996), p. 588.

9. *Our Daily Bread*, July 23 (Grand Rapids, MI: Zondervan Publishing House, 1959).

10. John W. Cowart, *People Whose Faith Got Them into Trouble—Stories of Costly Discipleship* (Downers Grove, IL: InterVarsity Press, 1990), pp. 55-64.

11. William Barclay, *The Letters to the Philippians, Colossians, and Thessalonians*, revised edition (Philadelphia, PA: The Westminster press, 1975), p. 37.

12. Charles Swindoll, *Improving Your Serve* (Waco, TX: Word Publishers, 1982), p. 34.

13. See Elizabeth George, *Women Who Loved God—A Devotional Walk with the Women of the Bible* (Eugene, OR: Harvest House Publishers, 1999).

14. Paul Lee Tan, *Encyclopedia of 7,700 Illustrations* (Winona Lake, IN: BMH Books, 1979), p. 817.

15. D. L. Moody, *Notes from My Bible and Thoughts from My Library* (Grand Rapids, MI: Baker Book House, 1979), p. 315.

16. Barclay, *Letters to the Philippians, Colossians, and Thessalonians*, pp. 66-67.

17. Charles F. Pfeiffer and Everett F. Harrison, *The Wycliffe Bible Commentary* (Chicago, IL: Moody Press, 1973), p. 1328.

18. Ralph P. Martin, *Tyndale New Testament Commentaries—The Epistle of Paul to the Philippians* (Grand Rapids, MI: William B. Eerdmans Publishing Company, 1976), 168.

19. D. L. Moody, *Notes from My Bible and Thoughts from My Library*, p. 316.

20. Barclay, *Letters to the Philippians, Colossians, and Thessalonians*, p. 79.

21. Drawn from Martin, *The Epistle of Paul to the Philippians*, p. 171.

22. Keith L. Brooks, *Philippians—The Epistle of Christian Joy* (Chicago, IL: The Moody Bible Institute of Chicago, 1963), p. 38.

23. Norman Grubb, *C. T. Studd* (Grand Rapids, MI: Zondervan Publishing House, 1946), pp. 50-51, 66-69.

24. Ibid., pp. 66-69

25. Barclay, *Letters to the Philippians, Colossians, and Thessalonians*, p. 87.

26. Hendriksen, *Exposition of Philippians*, p. 92.

27. Drawn from Hendriksen, *Exposition of Philippians*, p. 92.

28. Ibid., pp. 127-28.

29. Morgan, *Life Applications*, p. 351.

30. Hendriksen, *Exposition of Philippians*, p. 204.

Bibliography

Barclay, William. *The Letters to the Philippians, Colossians, and Thessalonians*, revised edition. Philadelphia: The Westminster Press, 1975.

Brooks, Keith L. *Philippians—The Epistle of Christian Joy*. Chicago: The Moody Bible Institute of Chicago, 1963.

Henry, Matthew. *Commentary on the Whole Bible*. Peabody, MA: Hendrickson Publishers, 1996.

Hendricksen, William. *New Testament Commentary—Exposition of Philippians*. Grand Rapids, MI: Baker Book House, 1975.

Jamieson, Robert, A. R. Fausset, and David Brown. *Commentary on the Whole Bible*. Grand Rapids, MI: Zondervan Publishing House, 1973.

Jensen, Irving L. *Philippians—A Self-Study Guide*. Chicago: The Moody Bible Institute of Chicago, 1973.

MacArthur, John. *The MacArthur Study Bible*. Nashville, TN: Word Publishing, 1997.

Martin, Ralph P. *Tyndale New Testament Commentaries—The Epistle of Paul to the Philippians*. Grand Rapids, MI: William B. Eerdmans Publishing Company, 1976.

Pfeiffer, Charles F. and Everett F. Harrison. *The Wycliffe Bible Commentary*. Chicago: Moody Press, 1973.

Tenney, Merrill C. *Zondervan Pictorial Encyclopedia of the Bible*. Grand Rapids, MI: Zondervan Publishing House, 1975.

Walvoord, John F. *Philippians—Triumph in Christ*. Chicago: Moody Press, 1977.

About the Author

Elizabeth George is a bestselling author who has more than four million books in print. She is a popular speaker at Christian women's events. Her passion is to teach the Bible in a way that changes women's lives. For information about Elizabeth's speaking ministry, to sign up for her mailings, or to purchase her books visit her website:

www.ElizabethGeorge.com

BIBLE STUDIES *for* BUSY WOMEN

Character Studies

Old Testament Studies

New Testament Studies

A WOMAN AFTER GOD'S OWN HEART® BIBLE STUDIES

*E*lizabeth takes women step-by-step through the Scriptures, sharing wisdom she's gleaned from more than 30 years as a women's Bible teacher.

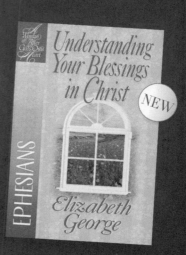

NEW

Books by Elizabeth George

- Beautiful in God's Eyes
- Finding God's Path Through Your Trials
- Following God with All Your Heart
- Life Management for Busy Women
- Loving God with All Your Mind
- A Mom After God's Own Heart
- Quiet Confidence for a Woman's Heart
- The Remarkable Women of the Bible
- Small Changes for a Better Life
- Walking with the Women of the Bible
- A Wife After God's Own Heart
- Windows into the Word of God
- A Woman After God's Own Heart®
- A Woman After God's Own Heart® Deluxe Edition
- A Woman After God's Own Heart®—A Daily Devotional
- A Woman After God's Own Heart® Collection
- A Woman's Call to Prayer
- A Woman's High Calling
- A Woman's Walk with God
- A Young Woman After God's Own Heart
- A Young Woman After God's Own Heart—A Devotional
- A Young Woman's Call to Prayer
- A Young Woman's Guide to Making Right Choices
- A Young Woman's Walk with God

Study Guides

- Beautiful in God's Eyes Growth & Study Guide
- Finding God's Path Through Your Trials Growth & Study Guide
- Following God with All Your Heart Growth & Study Guide
- Life Management for Busy Women Growth & Study Guide
- Loving God with All Your Mind Growth & Study Guide
- A Mom After God's Own Heart Growth & Study Guide
- The Remarkable Women of the Bible Growth & Study Guide
- Small Changes for a Better Life Growth & Study Guide
- A Wife After God's Own Heart Growth & Study Guide
- A Woman After God's Own Heart® Growth & Study Guide
- A Woman's Call to Prayer Growth & Study Guide
- A Woman's High Calling Growth & Study Guide
- A Woman's Walk with God Growth & Study Guide

Children's Books

- God's Wisdom for Little Girls
- A Little Girl After God's Own Heart

Books by Jim & Elizabeth George

- God Loves His Precious Children
- God's Wisdom for Little Boys
- A Little Boy After God's Own Heart

Books by Jim George

- The Bare Bones Bible® Handbook
- The Bare Bones Bible® Handbook for Teens
- The Bare Bones Bible® Bios
- The Bare Bones Bible® Facts
- A Husband After God's Own Heart
- A Man After God's Own Heart
- The Remarkable Prayers of the Bible
- A Young Man After God's Own Heart